A man comes across an ancient enemy, beaten and left for dead. He lifts the wounded man onto the back of a donkey and takes him to an inn to tend to the man's recovery. Jesus tells this story and instructs those who are listening to "go and do likewise."

Likewise books explore a compassionate, active faith lived out in real time. When we're skeptical about the status quo, Likewise books challenge us to create culture responsibly. When we're confused about who we are and what we're supposed to be doing, Likewise books help us listen for God's voice. When we're discouraged by the troubled world we've inherited, Likewise books encourage us to hold onto hope.

In this life we will face challenges that demand our response. Likewise books face those challenges with us so we can act on faith.

LIKEWISE.   *Go and do.*

Karen E. Sloan

FOREWORD BY John Ortberg

FLIRTING WITH
MONASTICISM

Finding God on Ancient Paths

IVP Books

An imprint of InterVarsity Press
Downers Grove, Illinois

InterVarsity Press
P.O. Box 1400, Downers Grove, IL 60515-1426
World Wide Web: www.ivpress.com
E-mail: email@ivpress.com

InterVarsity Press® is the book-publishing division of InterVarsity Christian Fellowship/USA®, a student movement
active on campus at hundreds of universities, colleges and schools of nursing in the United States of America, and a
member movement of the International Fellowship of Evangelical Students. For information about local and regional
activities, write Public Relations Dept., InterVarsity Christian Fellowship/USA, 6400 Schroeder Rd., P.O. Box 7895,
Madison, WI 53707-7895, or visit the IVCF website at <www.intervarsity.org>.

Design: by Cindy Kiple
Cover images: Convent: Adalberto Rios Szalay/Sexto Sol/Getty Images
            Candles: istockphoto.com
Interior images: Lila Jihanian

ISBN-10: 0-8308-3602-0
ISBN-13: 978-0-8308-3602-4

Printed in the United States of America ∞

Library of Congress Cataloging-in-Publication Data

Sloan, Karen E., 1976-
   Flirting with monasticism: finding God on ancient paths / Karen E.
   Sloan.
      p. cm.
   ISBN-13: 978-0-8308-3602-4 (pbk.: alk. paper)
   ISBN-10: 0-8308-3602-0 (pbk.: alk. paper)
   1. Monastic and religious life. 2. Spiritual life—Catholic Church.
   3. Spiritual life—Christianity. I. Title
   BX2435.S56 2006
   255'.2—dc22

                                                                2006030077

P	18	17	16	15	14	13	12	11	10	9	8	7	6	5	4	3	2	1
Y	20	19	18	17	16	15	14	13	12	11	10	09	08	07	06			

To my mom, Linnea,

for many years of reasons,

but mostly because you try

and to the

Order of Friars Preachers

contemplare et contemplata

aliis tradere

CONTENTS

FOREWORD

I didn't know.

I grew up in the church. I knew that I was supposed to pray and read the Bible. I knew that I was supposed to believe the right stuff and attend church and avoid certain kinds of sin. I knew that often people who were quite devoted to these practices did not seem to be much more loving or joyful than folks who were outside the church altogether.

But I did not know that across the centuries there have been brilliant and sensitive people who have given ruthless experimentalism and careful thought to the process by which human minds and hearts can be transformed by God. I did not know that across the centuries there have been sensitive souls who have banded together in community and devoted their lives to the pursuit of union with God.

Karen Sloan knows. She has spent considerable time and effort to learn about the practice of monastic life and what it might teach those of us on the other side of habits and cells.

Dallas Willard said once that those who pursue depth get breadth thrown in, but those who pursue only breadth get neither breadth nor depth. Because human nature is a constant across the centuries, certain practices are always needed for its change. Learning about them in depth from the Dominicans prepares us to see them broadly in other traditions and garb.

So happy reading! The transformation you're flirting with may be your own.

John Ortberg
Pastor
Menlo Park Presbyterian Church

PREFACE

Flirting

I'm not someone who can offer wise advice about flirting with anyone, monastic or otherwise. Even thinking about it makes me blush with embarrassment. I can tell you confidently, however, that flirting with the practices of monasticism often leads to amazing dates with God.

I keep finding people who are curious, as I am, about life in a monastic order. As part of an order, members' lives are organized around shared commitments and structures; these enable them to live far more faithfully than each member would be able to on their own. What is it that people in orders know about being with God (contemplation) and doing with God (action) that leads them to commit to a life so distinct from nearly everyone else? *??*

Not everyone is called to live a monastic life, but many of us would be blessed if we were able to live more monastically.

This is a story about what an outsider can discover from being around those in the Dominican order, though not what one would know from living within the order. There is more to life in an order than my glimpses into the public aspects of what they do. As an outsider writing about the Dominican world, I have intentionally chosen to not attempt a critique. The picture I have painted of Dominicans through telling my story leaves out some of the less pleasant aspects of life in an order.

And there is a much wider Catholic world that extends beyond Dominican orders. Thus many of my experiences with the Dominican order are not uniquely Dominican, but reflect their connection to the larger world of orders and the Catholic church in general. My apologies if I have neglected these connections, however, it is primarily through the Dominicans that I have been privileged to explore the worlds of Catholics and of orders.

Being a woman is another barrier in my journey; there is much I don't instinctively grasp, in general, about men and groups of men.

Welcome to this story. My prayer is that through the sharing of it, you and your community would desire to explore these paths further—that what has captured my heart would also tug at your heart.

1

FINDING GOD ON ANCIENT
AND NOT-SO-ANCIENT PATHS

*M*y life has taken some very unexpected turns in the last year. These days, I'm spending a lot of time around men who are dressed as if they were living in medieval Europe.

But it's not only their clothes that are different. It is their distinctive way of living that, the unusual outfit aside, draws me to find out more about them. Crossing paths with these men, Dominicans, a little over a year ago awoke and shaped spiritual longings in me, which previously I had not known were inside. This is not the spiritual path on which I started.

PATHWAYS

Growing up in an evangelical megachurch was a blessing of incredible teaching and exceptional music. God drew me in through the church's summer day camp program for elementary school kids. In the midst of flashy youth programs, I continued to encounter Jesus and learned to value prayer, Bible study and evangelism. After attending three one-hour sessions on Sunday afternoons in the spring of ninth grade, I was baptized and welcomed as an official member of the church. During short-term mission trips to Mexico and poor urban areas nearby, the Holy Spirit moved my heart to focus my life on things of lasting significance.

I left the San Francisco Bay Area upon graduating from high

school to go to a small college in the Los Angeles area. Immediately I connected with the college's Christian fellowship. The group was small, and their weekly meetings sometimes tedious, yet their faith was extremely vibrant. As older students in the group actively reached out to me, I was able to observe their faith up-close. The example of their lives, of having a lived faith at the center of their college pursuits, challenged me to deepen my own spiritual life. And the experience gave me a hunger for a richer life of spiritual commitment—a monastic life.

Of course, none of us referred to ourselves as monastic. We were a mix of frozen-chosen mainline denominations, liturgy-loving Catholics and hand-raising Pentecostals. We watched—and were inspired by—movies about orders such as *The Mission* and *Brother Sun, Sister Moon,* but we were just a campus Christian fellowship group seeking to be faithful.

There was lots of prayer.

There was lots of Bible study.

There was lots of loving our neighbors.

There wasn't a whole lot of dating.

This way of living was incredibly rewarding, and ever since that time I have been seeking a life in a Christian community of prayer and service.

SEARCHING IN ADULTHOOD

When I finished college I said farewell to the Christian fellowship. Returning home to the San Francisco Bay Area, I also returned to the evangelical megachurch. I got connected to Bible studies and prayer gatherings, which led to the serendipitous blessing of gaining a prayerful housemate, Michelle. Unsure about exactly where my life was heading, our nightly prayer times opened both of us to future directions that neither had expected. After much discernment, our time as roommates came to an end: Michelle married a wonderful man, and I drove to Los Angeles to begin seminary.

The transition to graduate school opened up a number of uncertainties. While looking for housing during orientation, I slept on friends' couches and lived out of a suitcase. But I registered for classes and found a small apartment that ended up being my home for the next five years. I began to settle into some rhythms of life. Within months I ended up at a delightful small, multiethnic Presbyterian church that became my spiritual home throughout my seminary education.

Seminary brought wonderful friendships into my life. I was stretched in charismatic experiences of God by being around students from Vineyard churches. Spending time with those from Episcopal churches expanded my contemplative experience of God. Being in seminary also taught me what the "Presbyterian Church (USA)" label, which I had seen on the sign of the church I was raised in, would actually mean for becoming a pastor in that denomination.

Coming to the end of my graduate education, I was getting closer to my thirtieth birthday and confused about where my life was headed. In my first year of seminary I had received an overwhelming confirmation of a call to pastor as an ordained Minister of Word and Sacrament and that sense of call provided needed encouragement in difficult moments over the years leading to my graduation. But with my seminary studies completed, my denomination's ordination process nearly done and applications sent out for seemingly countless pastor positions, I still wasn't seeing any doors open up for me. In applications and interviews I shared about my core passions—a longing for authentic community, an attraction to spiritual formation and a desire to bring together mission, evangelism and social justice—but received almost no response.

It didn't feel like anything substantial was happening in my life. I felt stuck. To cover my expenses as weeks grew to months of waiting, I ended up in an amiable job in local government. Although I enjoyed working with the city hall staff, the job involved reviewing reports about garbage tonnage and processing complaints related to the city's sewer project. It didn't seem like an ideal application of the hours I had spent studying Presbyterian polity. I wondered, *God, what are you doing? How can this path be going anywhere?*

AN ORDERED LIFE

Looking back over this year, I know it was not the meaningless time that it sometimes felt like. There was actually a lot happening in the small rhythms of my days. Through a series of quite unexpected circumstances, I was slowly becoming acquainted with the Dominicans, a medieval order of Catholic friars. The very things that my spiritual path had led me to desire, and the things I was failing to find in my job search, I found at the center of Dominican life.

To be a Dominican is to live all of life in community with other Dominicans.

To be a Dominican is to be devoted to prayer and study.

To be a Dominican is to preach the good news of Jesus Christ in words and deeds.

The world of those in the order is obviously different in many ways from the evangelical world. Yet observing the practices of friars in the Dominican order, and then getting to know friars themselves, has led continually to surprising connections with my spiritual journey.

So who exactly are the Dominicans? Around eight hundred years ago, Dominic de Guzman gave his life to form a new order in the Catholic Church. Moved by the need for preaching to call people to faith, he gathered and trained communities of  priests and brothers to follow a monastic rule of prayer and materialistic simplicity as itinerant preachers of the gospel. Though monastic in their spirituality, the Dominicans did not follow the tradition of monks, whose commitments include staying in one (usually secluded) place. The Dominicans were friars, not monks; they lived in and traveled to urban centers as they preached the gospel. Ministering in urban settings often required intelligent and systematic explanations of faith, causing the well-educated Dominic to make sure those in the order studied extensively at the best universities in Europe. The fruit of Dominic's life-work, forming people for the preaching of the gospel through being a part of the order that would later be referred to as Dominican, is still present today. Around the globe, there are communities of Dominicans who continue to lay down their lives in obedience to the calling of God to become a Dominican.

Joining the order is a process that involves extensive formation, including many years of education. The first step is entering the novitiate, a year-long period of leaving behind one's previous life to be deliberately formed as a novice in the Dominican order. Of the four components of Dominican life—prayer, community, study and ministry—the focus of the novitiate is on being plunged into Dominican community and rhythms of prayer. A Dominican novice passes a great deal of time in prayer: chanting Liturgy of the Hours, meditating during silent eucharistic adoration, participating in mass and saying the rosary.

In becoming acquainted with the order, I found myself experiencing their ways of prayer and their community. Though I'm obviously not a novice, this past year has been like something of a novitiate, an introduction to an ordered life.

If getting to know the Dominican order was so unexpected for me, how exactly did I end up on this path? It started with meeting Fran in the bustle of the Denver airport, a few months before he would enter the Dominican novitiate.

ENTERING: DINNER IN SEATTLE

"If you long for such formation, God will not fail to provide you opportunities to have that desire met," Fran declared with a quiet confidence. His words were very comforting, yet I had no sense of how prophetic they would turn out to be.

It was Friday evening, a few days before the Fourth of July. We were enjoying a simple meal at a wooden picnic table on a Seattle waterfront, talking about the novitiate world Fran would enter in a few weeks. The air was cool and the sky gray, typical for Seattle even in July. Obviously well-fed birds kept coming by in search of food.

Even as someone who had just finished several years of seminary training, I had difficulty relating to the process Fran described. Even before he would begin his seminary studies, he would have an entire year with the Dominicans to prayerfully discern his vocational call-

ing. I was a bit jealous; to be able to spend a year in this kind of focused spiritual formation sounded wonderful. (A year later a Dominican priest would ask me incredulously, "You mean you just *showed
up* at seminary and started studying?")

Fran was beginning a journey that sounded fascinating. My curi-
osity aroused, I wondered what this idealized experience would actually be like in lived reality. So Fran invited me to visit him at the
Catholic church in San Francisco that would be his home for the upcoming novice year. Given that I traveled from my home in Los Angeles to the San Francisco Bay Area every couple months to spend
time with my family, it seemed unexpectedly possible that I would
see Fran again.

I had met Fran only a month before, both of us on our way to a
conference. I had picked up my luggage at the Denver airport bag-
gage claim and found my way to a small group of people waiting for
the shuttle van to the conference center. Everyone rapidly introduced themselves. When I turned and met Fran, I was startled and
flustered by his good looks. Lacking any skills in flirting, and
knowing nothing about him, I told myself to put aside this initial
response. Yet at the conference we were placed in the same small
group and got to know each other in conversations during that
time.

Fran was in the final stages of wrapping up his career in ocean en-
gineering and preparing to become a Dominican friar. Raised in the
Catholic church, Fran became more alive to a personal faith while
working on a research ship in his mid-twenties. This led him to become actively involved at a Dominican church in Seattle. Though accepted into graduate programs across the country, he remained in Seattle to study at the University of Washington and to consider the

MEETING A MOVIE STAR

Perhaps like me you have a secret, or sometimes not-so-secret,
place in your heart where you hold an infatuation with an actor
or model that you find gorgeous. Over the years, various famous men
have held this spot in my heart. A certain actor had been the lead
in several recent blockbuster movies that I had seen,
and while I would have been too embarrassed to admit it, his appearance
made me swoon. The similarity of Fran's appearance
to this actor is uncanny; that's why I was so startled when I met him.
I tried not to blush as I shook his hand. I blamed my dazed state on having
just gotten off a several-hour plane flight. But inside all I could think was,
Wow, I'm meeting a movie star. When he said his name was Fran,
I thought, No it's not. But the blockbuster movies I was thinking of
gave way to the beginning of a less well-known movie, Strictly Ballroom, in
which a lead character introduces herself as "Fran . . . just Fran."

Mercifully, Fran wandered off from our group, allowing me to collect myself.
Then as the van arrived to take our group to the conference center,
a man asked, "Wait—isn't a guy missing?"
A woman said, "You mean the actor?" Everyone laughed;
apparently his familiar appearance had been noticed by all.
As Fran returned to our group, another man introduced himself and said,
"You're not quite as tall as you appear in the movies."

Eventually Fran's appearance ceased to startle me. However, these days,
instead of seeing Fran and thinking of the actor, seeing the actor
now makes me think of Fran.

growing desire in his heart to serve others through joining an order. Fran impressed me by his consistent concern for others' needs. In formal and informal gatherings for conversations, while at meals and overseeing a several-mile hike, his demeanor and actions were amazingly attentive to those around him. But given our different geographic locations and professional pursuits, I had no intention of remaining in touch with him. Fran was just one of many quality people I am grateful to meet at such conferences.

I had not expected to see Fran anytime so soon. Yet four weeks later I was in the city where he lived and had been to his church.

Being in Seattle that weekend was a last-minute whim. Earlier that week I had finally ended several weeks of phone tag with a good friend from college, Brook, whom I hadn't seen since his wedding a few years earlier. Now he and his wife, Susan, had a young son and were pregnant with another. Every time we spoke on the phone Brook would ask me when he should pick me up at the Seattle airport. I was touched by Brook and Susan's kindness and didn't want to continue to refuse their hospitality. So when I remembered that I had a frequent flyer ticket available for use and realized my schedule would allow me to take a few days to visit Seattle, I said, "Brook, what if I did actually fly up tomorrow for the holiday weekend?" Brook assured me that if I could get myself to the airport, his family would take care of all the other arrangements for the visit—meals, the use of their cars, and so forth.

With several days free to explore Seattle, I emailed everyone I knew in that city to find out what adventures would be possible. I visited several churches, had many good meals, watched an ultimate Frisbee tournament and even hiked on Mount  Rainer. Fran's response to my email was to invite me to join him for the evening mass at his church and then have dinner together.

ORDERS, FRANCISCANS AND DOMINICANS

*Hundreds of orders and communities have arisen over the history
of the church. Some have been around for centuries;
others are just beginning to form. Some exist only in memory.
When someone today considers joining an order, it usually involves an
element of exploration. Fran researched both the
Franciscan and the Dominican orders.*

*Dominic, the founder of the Dominicans, and Francis, the founder of the
Franciscans, both lived and formed their orders in the beginning of
thirteenth century. It is said that these two orders have
endured in church history as brothers—sometimes quarreling,
but more often taking a posture of supportive embrace for
each other's mendicant itinerant ministries.*

*The reasons for selecting an order or a community are as varied as those
who are in the process of exploration.
Somewhere in the fitness of personalities, an attraction to particular
distinctives and the call of God, the miracle of amazingly well-suited
matches does happen. This process is hardly instantaneous,
but rather the result of relationship-building over periods of time.*

After mass, we talked together over dinner, in a setting much
calmer than the frenetic conference a month earlier. Our conversation wandered. Noticing the persistent birds and recalling that
Francis of Asissi had frequently befriended birds, I made a remark

like, "Even though you share Saint Francis's name, I would not give these birds what they want." Fran smiled and told me he agreed. Then he told me about visiting Francis's hometown, Assisi, Italy, where he did end up sharing part of his lunch with birds near his bench. Prior to deciding on the Dominican Order, Fran had considered joining the Franciscans.

Somewhere in our conversation I happened to look directly into Fran's eyes, and an emotional tidal wave overwhelmed me. *Wow, this man is really wonderful.*

Instantly afraid of this feeling, my very next thought was, *Oh no, don't go there. Don't meet his eyes anymore and don't let him see what happened to you.* I tried to keep talking to Fran as if nothing had happened, but inside I was flustered. And this time it was much more than his appearance. *What do I do?*

Confused as our evening together concluded, I said goodbye to Fran and drove back to Brook and Susan's house. Though I talked with them briefly, soon I was alone. I knelt next to the couch I was sleeping on and prayed a prayer I would find myself continuing to pray in the coming months:

> Oh God, you know I don't have the words to pray about this situation. I don't know what to pray for. Something has shifted in my feelings for Fran, and I want to give all of this to you. It has been some years since anyone has evoked this kind of response in me. I do not want to just hide it away, afraid of being vulnerable. Help me know what to do. Bless Fran, lead him, give him wisdom.

LEAVING A FAMILIAR LIFE

Back in the routines of my life in Los Angeles, I found Fran still in my thoughts. Not only curious about his novitiate, I was now also curious about him. So a month after the Seattle trip I emailed Fran with dates that I would be in the San Francisco Bay Area visiting my family during August and September, and asked if it really would be possible to visit. In his thoughtful reply he let me know he would not yet be in the city during my first visit. "The second time you come back we will have recently come back from a retreat, where we prepare to receive the habit." He included a link to get directions to the church and suggested that I visit for their late-afternoon services.

He never received my response to his email, a couple weeks later, saying that I was planning on coming by for Evening Prayer and mass. Though I did not learn this until later on in the year, once men enter formation with the Dominicans they are fairly cloistered for the first year, meaning their interactions with the larger world are extremely limited. While they can send and receive mail and occasionally make phone calls, email is something they give up completely during the novice year. With the recent dramatic rise in communication technologies, such as text messaging and instant messenger, and web services like blogs and social networks, being removed from these things can be jarring for entering novices. Only after completing the novitiate are the communication restrictions eased. A young brother, who became a novice right after finishing college, told me as I wrote down my email for him, "Thank you. Now that the novitiate is done we are finally rejoining the civilized world."

If the novitiate had not been located in a place I could easily personally visit, and if I had not had the time in September to enjoy a beautiful day of roaming around San Francisco, it is very likely I would never have communicated with Fran again. And he would not have become my starting point for learning about the Dominican order.

CIRCUMSTANCES OF GEOGRAPHY

Confused by how Fran and I were able to cross paths in such a variety of places? So much of this story would not have happened if the circumstances of geography had been different.

We were both living in the cities where we had completed graduates studies, Fran in Seattle and I in Los Angeles. Independently deciding to attend an ecumenical conference, we met in Colorado.

A month later while in Los Angeles, Brook invited me to visit his family in Seattle. During this trip, Fran and I spent a few hours together, and he shared about his upcoming move to San Francisco, inviting me to visit him there.

Two months later, during a visit with my mom and a necessary meeting for my career, I went to see Fran's new living situation. Now he was Brother Emmanuel, living in an all-male community dressed in white habits. I was uncertain if I should visit him again. Asking him about this, he encouraged me to visit.

That fall, as I returned to visit my mom in the San Francisco Bay Area at the end of September, and again at Thanksgiving and Christmas, I stopped by the Dominican church in San Francisco.

The primary reason for that particular visit to the Bay Area was the final meeting with my ordination committee. In a Wednesday morning meeting I preached a sermon and answered some questions. They voted to approve my readiness for ministry, certifying that I had completed all the requirements to be ordained. That weekend I was spending time with friends from college, but Thursday and Friday were unexpectedly open on my schedule. And even for the Bay Area, the weather was incredibly beautiful. There wasn't a cloud in the sky over San Francisco, and the warm sunshine kept temperatures in the high 80s. Sitting around on Thursday, I decided I might as well craft specific plans for the next day. My sister agreed to drop me off at the train station during her lunch break from work.

Arriving at the end of the train line by the Giants baseball stadium, I pulled out my map, put on lots of sunblock, and started walking. I passed by shops on Market Street and wandered through Chinatown, then made a pilgrimage to the labyrinths at Grace Cathedral. After calmly walking the indoor labyrinth I quickly perused the cathedral's gift store; I didn't have time to linger if I was going to get to the Dominican church in time for the start of Evening Prayer.

I was a bundle of nervous excitement. I had little idea of what to expect as I arrived at the huge church. I spotted Fran among the men in white at the front of the sanctuary and sat in a pew toward the mid-

dle of the church, watching them offer Evening Prayer. It became apparent that mass would take place in the side chapel, so I moved to a pew just a few rows behind where Fran had sat. He hadn't noticed that I was there.

My sermon to the ordination committee had been drawn from Numbers 6:22-27, and I had preached on the powerful impact of speaking blessing on others. So when I came forward to receive a blessing from the priest as he was serving the Eucharist to the congregation, I was deeply moved. He put down the consecrated host, reached out his hand to touch my forehead, and said, "May Almighty God bless you, the Father, the Son, and the Holy Spirit." Returning to my pew, I knew I had experienced what I had preached two days earlier, moving me to tears.

As the mass was ending I collected my emotions; I wanted to be certain I would have the chance to say hello to Fran before he left the chapel. Some of the people who had been at mass were now pulling out rosaries and gathering to recite it together. "Hail Mary, full of grace . . ." I went up to where Fran was standing and said, "Hi Fran." He turned, looking surprised and then very glad to see me.

Now in the white habit of the order, he told me about the vestition ceremony the night before and other aspects of his new life. Eventually we ended up on the grounds outside the church, near a large statue of Mary. Talking together confirmed that what I had experienced in Seattle was not some fluke. When two other new novices joined us, Fran introduced them by the names they received during vestition, and indicated that I should now call him Brother Emmanuel. Though I didn't fathom the major change that had begun to take place, I could sense that the men were still adjusting to their new identities.

One of novices checked his watch and realized they were almost late to eucharistic adoration. With a hug, we said farewell and I watched the novices hurry back to the priory as I left in the other direction.

During the lengthy walk back to the train station, and on the train, I had a lot to think about. I hadn't noticed how much the temperature had cooled down after sunset, but not having a sweater didn't worry me. There were plenty of other uncertainties on my mind. In this visit I observed a beautiful church, experienced the Holy Spirit's presence in the liturgy and confirmed that my heart was still very much drawn to Fran. What does it mean when the man you want to get to know better is now a Dominican novice, a man who wears a white habit?

What had happened to Fran? Whoops, I mean, Brother Emmanuel?

2

VESTITION

Receiving the Habit

*E*ven if it would've helped me be less confused about Brother Emmanuel's new state of life, I could not have been present when he received the habit. While all the other major events in the years of becoming a Dominican are public ceremonies, vestition is a private moment that only Dominicans attend.

A year after Brother Emmanuel's vestition, I was talking with a kind Dominican priest, who has been in the order for decades, about how I was going to write about vestition. I was completely bewildered when he paused and earnestly asked me, "Have you ever been to one?" I had no idea how to respond. What is the right thing to say? "I'm not a Dominican"? "I've only become aware of the order in this last year"? "I'm female"? "I'm not Catholic"? We both sat still, neither one saying anything. Then, interpreting my puzzled face, he answered his own question—"No, of course not"—and started to describe what takes place.

THE BIG MOMENT OF BEGINNING

During the end of summer, just before vestition, those considering the Dominican order begin to live in community. While much discernment, prayer and reflection have led them to this point, these weeks—called postulancy—are a key time of deep consideration whether they will actually move forward with the process of formally entering the order.

In vestition, each man is welcomed in an elaborate process of leaving behind the old and taking on a new identity. In Brother Emmanuel's province, vestition usually occurs during Night Prayer, after the Scripture reading. The novice master invites the postulates forward: "Those who are to receive the habit of the Order of Preachers please come forward." The postulants silently stand before the regional head of the order, the provincial, who asks their intentions: "What do you seek?"

Affirming their desire to begin the novice year, the postulates respond by saying, "God's mercy, and yours." They then prostrate their bodies on the ground, face down, hands extended in the form of a cross.

The provincial invites the gathered community to kneel, as everyone shares in a time of silent prayer: "Let us pray for our brothers who are asking to be received into our Order, that the Divine Master may grant them the abundance of his Spirit and the consolation of his peace."

Then the novice master invites the community to stand as the provincial prays over the prostrate postulants, with the gathered community responding with "Amen." Following the time of prayer in such a vulnerable posture of submission, the provincial says, "Arise," and the postulants rise to their feet, returning to where they had been sitting when vestition began.

Once everyone is seated, the provincial may address the postulants and the gathered community about what is required to be a part of the Order. Then the novice master invites the postulants to stand,

and the provincial has the postulants affirm their intentions by asking several questions.

> Provincial: Is it your firm intention to walk faithfully in new-
> ness of life?
> Postulants: It is, with God's help and yours.
>
> Provincial: Do you wish to follow the Lord Jesus according to
> the evangelical plan of blessed Dominic?
> Postulants: I do, with God's help and yours.
>
> Provincial: Do you therefore wish to be received into our Order,
> to undertake our way of life in perfect regular observance?
> Postulants: I do, with God's help and yours.
>
> Provincial: May the Lord, who has begun this good work in
> you, bring it to perfection.
> Everyone: Amen.

Each man then takes off the white dress shirt he is wearing. One by one each man, in a white tee-shirt and dark slacks, comes forward to kneel before the provincial. The provincial lowers the habit over the postulant, leaving the capuce of the habit up to cover the man's head. Returning to his seat, each man silently waits for the other postulates to be clothed in the habit.

Each man, now wearing the habit, returns one by one to the provincial to receive the name he will be called as a part of the order: "In the world you were known as _____, in the Order you will be called Brother _____." He is blessed with holy water by the provincial, who then lowers the man's capuce. With an uncovered head the novice is welcomed into the order with an embrace from the provincial. All the friars present then line up to embrace each novice in welcome, after which the community finishes Night Prayer.

A small reception follows to welcome the novices.

If a novice ever finds himself wondering how he ended up wearing a habit, the exhilaration of the vestition ceremony is a vivid memory of crossing over into life in the order. And as the months go by and the novices grow deeper into the Dominican life, they become noticeably more comfortable in wearing their habits.

In another U.S. Dominican province, vesition occurs as a part of Evening Prayer, just before dinner. There is a long-standing tradition that the dinner following vestition is spaghetti with meatballs and lots of red tomato sauce. A friar cannot live in fear of getting the white habit dirty, and this meal pretty much guarantees they will mess up their habit in the first hours of wearing it. One year a novice got more of this lesson than he expected; reaching across the table, he ended up with the entire lower half of his tunic's sleeve covered with tomato sauce. Oops.

A HABITED ORDER

While there are fewer than a thousand men in the Dominican order in the United States, their distinctive white and black habit make them easily identifiable. Watching them in action, negotiating the challenges that come with wearing habits, makes me thankful that my Christian journey has not led me to wear all white. At an ecumenical gathering, we had just sat down to dinner and were passing around the salad dressings, when the Dominican brother on my left selected the creamy raspberry vinaigrette and dropped a generous red spoonful onto his white habit. With a sigh of familiar misfortune, he grabbed a napkin and did what he could to blot the spill. Later in the evening I noticed that he had gotten a splotch of red wine on his habit as well. I asked if the order had special secrets for getting out stains. The brother responded with a smile: "You learn a few tricks," but he did not elaborate.

Monastic habits are dramatically different from men's fashions to-day. Nearly all orders in the Catholic church have unique, distinctive clothes, but in recent decades a number of orders have modernized their dress. However, the conventional wisdom among Dominican friars that keeps them from updating their habit is that "it's better to be medieval than thirty years out of date." Venturing into the Dominican order requires a willingness to be visually set apart from mainstream society and starkly identified as a person in an order.

At first glance a Dominican friar appears to be simply wearing a large amount of flowing white cloth, but their habit is actually fairly complex. "The back of your scapular is caught in your rosary" is in one sense a perfectly normal thing for me to say to Brother Emmanuel, but then again it illustrates the distinctiveness of the habit and the oddity of talking about it.

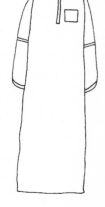

Underneath the habit, a friar dresses in everyday clothes—most typically slacks and a white dress shirt. One priest I know prefers jeans and flannel shirts; another priest told me, "I'm wearing shorts under this."

Over his everyday clothes a friar wears a long-sleeve, ankle-length tunic that covers his entire body, except for his head, hands and feet. The tunic resembles a shapeless white cotton nightgown, but a wide black or brown leather belt snugly cinctured around the waist gives it some shape. Hung on the belt are a long rosary and sometimes other, less sacred items, such as a cell phone.

Spending time around Dominicans occasionally causes me to want to wear a long, flowing skirt. Yet this impulse has never lasted longer than one day; I'm quickly reminded how much more convenient it is to wear pants. Moving about in the habit can be challenging, and while women are generally skilled in moving about with long skirts, novices face a steep learning curve. A Dominican recruiting website warns those considering the order that "it usually takes a few days to adjust to wearing the habit, and navigating stairs can be a tricky affair for the newly vested novice."

Beyond the tunic, belt and rosary, Dominican friars wear a a very long, narrow, rectangular piece of white fabric, called a scapular, over the front and back of the body, with a round opening in the middle for the head. Lacking any parallel to contemporary garments, it can seem impractical—especially to people standing next to them. One windy day I had to protect my face with my hands to prevent the back half of a friar's scapular from hitting my face. Yet the scapular has an important place in the history of the order: Mary directed the friars in a vision to wear it as a symbol of her protection and provision.

Crowning the habit is the capuce, a white hood whose fabric extends across the front of the tunic and scapular in a straight line just above the elbow and then forms a large triangle down the back.

From the back the capuce looks similar to the poncho-style shawls of women's fashion, with the addition of a hood. Yet other than keeping warm in a cold place, or novice silliness, the capuce is not usually used as a hood.

In addition to these white garments, Dominican attire also in-cludes a black cape and black capuce. These garments resulted in the friars being given the nickname "Black Friars" in some areas of Europe. The black garments are rarely worn in the United States, generally at only the most formal of occasions.

WEARING YOUR FAITH

There is not uniformity of opinion regarding how much of the time the habit should be worn. Friars cannot take for granted that they will blend into their surroundings, such as when the novice group arrived too late to find seats in a crowded church service. I realized with them, "It's not like you guys will be able to slip in unnoticed." Once I saw a priest rush into the church at the last minute before a prayer service. He had inadvertently tucked his tunic and scapular into the waist of his blue jeans. Even though he was fully clothed, he appeared to be unintentionally mooning the people behind him. A friar in the pew behind him soon let him know and everyone, especially the priest now fixing his tunic, suppressed laughter as we recited the opening prayer.

Some friars have wondered if wearing the habit can create unnecessary distance from other people, making them unapproachable. One time a startled student on a University of California campus, upon seeing a visiting group of friars in their flowing all-white outfits, asked the friars from a distance if they were members of the Ku Klux Klan.

A friar is permitted to wear everyday clothes when they are not in a ministry setting, but some friars have told me they appreciate the opportunities to talk about faith that arise when they are out around town in their habit. Part of the novice year is simply becoming accustomed to how people respond to them differently as a member of a habited order. Novices are regularly approached and interrupted, even when they are just seeking to pray quietly on their own. With their faith on such a public display, it becomes even more important to have a private chapel to serve as a refuge when needed.

Wearing a monastic habit can seem like such a mysterious thing, so other and foreign, and yet in so many ways the men in the habits are just that, men. Seeing the actual person of flesh inhabiting the unusual outfit can be a blessing, as my friend Todd discovered. Introducing Todd to Brother Emmanuel just before a prayer service, the two of them realized that they had grown up and played soccer in the same area. After prayer Todd realized how much more connected he felt during the prayer time; he now not only saw Brother Emmanuel as a novice in a white habit, but as a guy who at age fifteen had been playing a lot of soccer.

MY HABIT

Coming from a church where if a pastor wears clerical garb at all, it is only within the context of a worship service, I hadn't considered what it would mean to wear my faith so conspicuously. But during this year of being around Dominicans, I ended up in a vestition-type experience of my own.

I've been blessed to have several friends in training to become spiritual directors. As a part of their program they participated in monthly quiet days, a time set aside to be still in a beautiful setting and listen in extended times of prayer. Often I would join in on these days. When one of my friends, Michelle, decided to take a five-day quiet retreat at a Benedictine abbey just north of Los Angeles, I arranged my schedule to go with her.

There is so much of ourselves and of God that can be discovered through such times of intentional listening. Although I'm not in a place where I could easily enter into the stillness that those who go into a month, or months, of retreat might experience, my encounter at the abbey helped me grasp why people do that. During my first few days I enjoyed the stillness and praying the Divine Office with the monks, but nothing substantially insightful came to the surface. *Perhaps,* I thought, *I'm in a good place right now and there's not anything the Holy Spirit wants to draw to my attention.* On the afternoon of the fourth day of the retreat, it was obvious that I had needed those days of stillness and prayer before I could hear what I needed to hear.

What started coming to mind were memories of being a young child, when I would steal raw white sugar from the pink bag in the kitchen. I would hide the sugar in my room to eat it alone. This pattern went on for years; I took not just sugar but also raw pasta and other sweet treats that my mom would occasionally purchase. Everything would be carefully secreted back to my room, and I would munch on my haul privately, resupplying as needed. I was caught a few times, but I doubt anyone in my family was ever aware of the extent of what I was doing.

Eventually, without ever talking about the struggle with any other person, I stopped myself from sneaking and hiding food. As an active participant in my church's youth group, I felt convicted that what I was doing was wrong. But I never processed what that behavior pattern had been about; I simply put it behind me and forgot. So what did not go away was my impulse toward "emotional eating," attempting to use food to bring me comfort.

Overall I was a healthy eater, avoiding things like caffeine, soda and fast food, and making sure I ate plenty of fruits and vegetables.

A DIFFICULT CHILDHOOD, A HEALING JOURNEY

What was it that made me resort to stealing sugar as an elementary school child? My parents had a very difficult marriage. They both sought to be good parents, but it was not an emotionally easy home to grow up in. After nearly two decades of trying to make things work, they eventually divorced. Additionally, I often felt rejected at my socially intense elementary school, and I struggled with some learning disabilities, so life outside of my home was also distressing. It was when I finally had space from my home, especially in going away for college, that I would process the sadness and pain inside me. Through talking and praying with friends, and later working with a therapist, I began a journey of transformative healing.

Yet I gained a good deal of weight around my midsection during puberty, arriving at a body shape that would be relatively stable into adulthood. I didn't really worry that my body mass index was at the very high end, if not slightly over, "normal" weight range.

Then while I was in graduate school, my mom switched to a low-carb approach to eating. It had a dramatic impact on her overall health, and she became something of a low-carb evangelist. When I was around her it was easy to be inspired to want to eat this way. Actually living out that desire was another matter. The pull toward sugar was very strong. Knowing the temptation, I usually didn't keep sweets in my house. But that didn't stop me from thinking about going to the grocery store a few blocks from my house to get candy. Now at the abbey I could see that I formed these eating habits to cope with the stress of my childhood, and they had set a pattern running throughout the years that followed.

The night before going on the retreat with Michelle had been an unusually rough struggle with temptation. During the drive up to the monastery I told Michelle about wrestling with my "sugar monsters," wanting to put it out of my mind as we headed into the retreat. At the end of the retreat I shared with her about my memories of sugar stealing as a child; it was the first time I had ever talked about this part of my past, which I had hidden even from myself. Michelle was very gentle with my shame and embarrassment. In prayer together, I opened up this part of my life which I had been overlooking, inviting God in to lead me in a process of getting out of this pattern. I sensed that after years of prayerfully experiencing healing for the brokenness of which emotional eating was merely a symptom, I was now in a place of enough emotional health to be able to give up this coping mechanism.

Michelle continued to provide prayerful accountability, a listening ear and supportive hugs when we returned from the retreat. A whole year went by before my life calmed down enough for me to focus on being more consistently thoughtful about what I ate. I learned from my mom how to make better choices in food combinations, and more friends prayed with me about my changing habits. The damage done to my body from years of emotional eating slowly began to heal. And about four months into this new way of eating, I noticed that none of my pants were fitting anymore. My body mass index was moving toward the lower end of the normal weight range for my height. In the following weeks I found myself using something that had been hanging ignored in my closet for years: a belt.

Two months later I joined my mom for a vacation. Even though I had told her how my body shape was changing, she was surprised by the extent of the change. Most of my clothes were worn from years of living simply to avoid graduate school debt, and now they were also quite baggy. My mom took me to the mall to get me into some better threads. Trying on clothes was a shock. While I had been a petite 10, I had no idea what size I now was, so I kept trying smaller and smaller sizes until we sorted out that what now fit was a petite 2. No wonder my clothes had been baggy! Incredible sales and beautiful clothes kept us busy for much of our vacation.

Returning home with an entire new wardrobe, I went straight to work emptying my closet. Some things went directly to the trash, and I took seven bags to Goodwill. Even things I still liked had to go; none of it would fit as well as my new threads. Saying goodbye to clothes I still cared for, like my mandarin-style gray silk jacket, I felt a twinge of sadness. These items were still good, but I had to let them go. With the change that had taken place in my body, I would be deceiving myself if I held on to them. The new things I had been given were far better suited than the clothes I had shrunk out of for the path my life is now on.

Tossing the pink plastic hangers that had been acquired during my sugar stealing days and in my life for over twenty years, I hung up new clothes on new hangers in a freshly scrubbed closet. It was somewhat disorienting. In a matter of just a few days, everything that I had worn to present myself to the world was gone, and an entirely new set of things had replaced them. No longer did I look like a thrifty graduate student, now I dressed as a pastor. The new clothes moved me toward the next phase of my vocational life. As I completed the change of my closet, it felt right to say a brief prayer, that the items in the closet would not be just clothes that I wear but a part of living out God's purposes in my life.

My friend Jessica, several months after the clothing adventure, took me to a hairstylist who cut off my long unkempt hair into a much more stylish 'do. And, as she had done somewhat annually since she graduated from college, Jessica again patiently attempted to update my nearly nonexistent makeup skills. Jessica, who takes exceptional care of her hair and makeup, is pursuing a tug on her heart to become a cloistered Benedictine nun. It is ironic that even as she is helping me have a more polished personal appearance, her spiritual search may very well lead her into a life of wearing a traditional black habit with no makeup and her hair completely covered by a veil. Whether it's Jessica shopping for the black and white clothes she would need for her several month postulancy at a Benedictine abbey, Brother Emmanuel adjusting to his tunic and scapular, or me appreciating my new clothes, new hairstyle and new makeup, I know that God can be intimately involved in our personal appearance.

GETTING TO KNOW BROTHER EMMANUEL?

After my visit to the San Francisco Bay Area in early September, with no plans to return until Thanksgiving, I wrote a short letter to Brother Emmanuel. New habits aside, I thought, was it possible for me to get to know this man who was becoming much more than a passing fancy

to me? I decided to take that risk. My letter described experiencing how feelings between us changed while in Seattle, a change that was affirmed when I visited him in San Francisco. I had wanted to say something about my feelings, but the strangeness of the circumstances left me with many questions. Most of all, should I remain open to exploring where my feelings for him might lead? What were the constraints of his current state of life? Could I be a part of his life or was that impossible?

As a way of processing my emotions, writing the letter was very helpful. But I didn't plan on actually sending it. A few days later, however, my mom called to ask if I could make another trip to the Bay Area at the end of September for a family event. Suddenly I could talk with him in person. I wasn't going to miss this second opportunity.

I went to Brother Emmanuel's church on a Sunday morning, with hundreds of people coming to and from various masses. I didn't know how to find him. Eventually I found the church office and wrote him a note to say I had stopped by. I tucked the note in with the letter I had written and left it for him with the church's receptionist. As I walked down the priory steps to leave, I stumbled on the stairs, catching the notice of a novice walking up the steps. He told me to wait by the steps; he would  find Brother Emmanuel for me. The novice disappeared into the priory, I returned to the office to get my letter, and a moment later Brother Emmanuel appeared.

We sat down on a bench adjacent to the steps and chatted as we observed people leaving the church after the morning's concluding mass. Soon the busyness calmed, and uncertain about how long we would be able to talk together, I interrupted our chatting. "I have a very specific purpose in being here. I need to say something."

I was so nervous, I got stuck in inarticulate half-sentences. Wanting to spare me this struggle, he said, "I know what you're trying to say." He tried to steer the conversation in an easier direction, but I insisted, "I have to say it." Getting my nervousness under control, I did find words:

Me: "In Seattle something shifted between us."

Him: "Yes."

Me: "And if you were just a guy in my world I would want to spend time with you."

Him: *Smile*

Me: "I know you're not just a guy I know, that the circumstances of your life right now involves decision making that doesn't have anything to do with me, but I needed to say this."

DATING NOVICES?

Months after a friend told me that Catholic men considering entering orders are often encouraged to date, I figured out that this was not true for Brother Emmanuel's Dominican novitiate.
At the point of our "define the relationship" conversation, however, there was no one I knew other than him who could have told me this—and understandably, I wasn't going to ask him.

When I've recounted this story to friends, they interrupt at this point: "And? What did he say?!?"

Me: "He didn't really say anything. We sat on the bench and talked for another hour, until he had to leave for a meeting."

Them: "And you're okay with this?"

Me: "Well, what would he have said? I didn't really expect him to respond directly to my pointing out the attraction between us. My hope was that I would be able to express what I'm feeling, and I did that. Talking together after that didn't feel at all awkward. It was very enjoyable to spend that time together . . . wow, I really like him."

Them: "Really, you're okay with him not directly telling you how he feels about you?"

Me: "All right, it *is* unusual that he didn't say anything, but picture the scene. We're sitting outside an elaborate church on a warm, sunny day, and he's dressed in his Dominican habit. Occasionally, other men and women are walking by—also dressed in habits. While he hasn't taken any vows and I'm not clear how much freedom he has to be relating to me, he *is* at the beginning of a discernment process of whether or not he is called to join the order."

Them: "What does that mean?"

Me: "I don't really know what it means for him to be in this discernment process. I asked a Catholic friend who lives in another part of the country, and she told me that from what she's heard, men who are in discernment are often encouraged to date—that it's better for them to work through these feelings at this stage, before they have taken permanent vows."

Them: "And why exactly are you hopeful about him?"

Me: "In wrapping up our time together, I asked him directly, in a nonflirtatious way, 'Given what I said at earlier in our conversation, should I continue to visit you?' He paused to reflect for a moment, and then said, 'It brings me a lot of joy to see you. Yes, please visit.' Parting with a quick hug, I drove away in bliss."

Them: "So what happens now?"

Me: "I'm still shocked that after several years of being around a number of single men while in graduate school, not dating and being fairly peaceful about it, I've become so interested in a man. This doesn't happen for me that often, so I don't need to be in a rush. Our conversation that morning touched on a number of different topics—church history, spiritual formation, living in community, ministry—it left me with plenty to think about. And in an email from him just before he arrived in San Francisco, he asked for my address so he could write me, so I assume he can get letters. If I'm moved in the next few weeks to write up some further thoughts from our conversation, I'll send him a letter.

"Boy, I sure didn't expect all of this would be the outcome of meeting up at his church when I was visiting Seattle. Right now I'm really happy. I'm praying, asking God for insight on what to do."

3

THE LITURGY OF THE HOURS

Praying the Divine Office

*E*xploring Seattle on a Friday afternoon in July, I made my way to the Catholic church near the University of Washington to meet Fran for the evening mass. (He was still Fran at this point; this was two months prior to his entering the Dominican novitiate in San Francisco, where his name would change to Brother Emmanuel.) I arrived half an hour early and toured the church, settling down in a pew near the front to continue reading *The Way of a Pilgrim*, an Orthodox classic about a Russian pilgrim who learns to pray the Jesus prayer. Off to the side of the church I noticed a group of people who had started singing, or something. It wasn't clear to me what they were doing; perhaps they were practicing for the weekend services?

When Fran arrived, I asked about the group. His matter-of-fact reply: "Oh, they're praying Evening Prayer, a prayer service of the Liturgy of the Hours."

MONKS AT PRAYER

Once I realized what was going on, I lit up. The first time I had found myself in such a prayer service, years before, was like nothing else I had previously experienced. During my first year at seminary I took an elective course called "Spirituality in Everyday Life" with Jen, a friend and a regular prayer partner. A central part of the class included studying how the Rule of St. Benedict shapes the rhythms of life for a community of Benedictine women. Inspired by the class and her own reading of Kathleen Norris's *The Cloister Walk*, Jen suggested we spend several days on retreat at a monastery during our spring break.

I found Jen's idea of visiting a monastery unusual, but I committed to go on the condition that she would make all the arrangements. She called at least twenty places before deciding on a community near San Diego. We finished our classes and drove off in her car (I had just gashed my front right tire on a surprisingly jagged curb outside her apartment), somewhat nervous about what we were getting ourselves into.

An hour and a half later we were driving up the twisty road that leads to the abbey, enchanted by the beauty of the grounds. As guests at this abbey, the two of us would do individual retreats and join in five daily prayer services. Being hospitable is a central hallmark of the Benedictine way of life; as their rule instructs them, "Let all guests who arrive be received like Christ." We felt that hospitality as we checked in, and it quickly put us at ease.

As we had learned in class, a monk's life is a balance of prayer, work and rest. As the Benedictine Rule coaches, "Whatever good work you begin to do, beg of Him with most earnest prayer to perfect it." Between periods of work and rest, this specific community of monks gathers five times daily—5:30 a.m., 7:00 a.m., 11:00 a.m., 5:00 p.m., 8:00 p.m.—for prayers in the chapel (with a full mass at 11:00 a.m.). Anyone is welcome to participate in these services, called collectively the divine office. So we settled in our retreat rooms and then headed over to the chapel to wait for the 5:00 p.m. service to start. Another guest guided us to the correct page in the prayer book so we could follow along.

Men wearing the black habit of Benedictines processed in and began to sing back and forth, alternately standing, sitting and bowing. It was all a bit confusing, yet reading along in the prayer book, I realized that nearly all of what they were saying came directly from Scripture. The majority of the service was praying the psalms.

In the past I have been a prayer snob. I considered scripted prayers a cop out and instead practiced extemporaneous intercessory prayer. Experiencing the prayerfulness of the monks, however, I had to repent of my arrogance. By the 8:00 p.m. service I was ready to attempt to chant along with them, and by participating in more services the next day I gained a solid sense of the basics.

NEED A RETREAT?

Spiritual considerations aside, monastic retreats are usually fairly economical: included in the cost is a private room, meals and wonderful prayer services. Whenever anyone mentions to me that they need a break, I encourage them to explore doing a retreat at a monastery.

The simple beauty of the chapel, the organ music accompanying the chanting and the Scripture-infused community prayer were incredibly moving, a great blessing. The months around the retreat were a very difficult season for me as I worked through a painful part of my past. Yet returning to Los Angeles after a few days of this routine, I felt incredibly refreshed. (It helped that the food was excellent and that several monks kept us laughing by telling corny jokes.)

SINGING THE SAME SONG

There was nothing comparable to the divine office in my church experience—no structure for gathering several times a day to be in prayer and Scripture. Instead, I had been given repeated instruction in the importance of having a "personal quiet time," time set aside each day to read the Bible and pray. Even after many years of being a Christian, I am not as disciplined in this practice as I would hope to be. Apart from the regular support and accountability of Christian community, I struggle to live faithfully in isolation. Having experienced Liturgy of the Hours, I began to long for a more regular experience of this kind of prayer, but other than visiting monasteries, I had no idea how I could go about finding such a community.

The quasi-community of singing along with the songs on Christian radio stations every morning and evening as I drove to and from work was a lesser substitute. A song by Chris Rice, "Other Side of the Radio," reflects on this experience and resonated with me:

> Cause it's you and me singing the same song right now
> And maybe this will bring us together somehow
> And maybe there's a million people all singing along.

"Other Side of the Radio" would remind me that by singing along to this song I was connected, in a sense, to everyone else who sang along to it. Liturgy of the Hours reflects a similar longing: individuals and groups praying along with communities around the globe—countless numbers of people in a million places, in many languages, praying with Jesus through the same psalms. I was not alone when I participated in these prayers.

I acquired *The Glenstal Book of Prayer* and tried praying its simplified divine office on my own, in an attempt to join in with this stream of prayer. But distractions abounded. Some people have the discipline to pray Liturgy of the Hours on their own, but that is not me. Many people find it easier to maintain a prayer routine in the presence of at least a few others. Would I ever find a community that I could join regularly for praying Liturgy of the Hours?

DOMINICANS IN MY NEIGHBORHOOD!

The practice of Evening Prayer at the Dominican church in Seattle was nothing remarkable to Fran. He told me that generally all Catholic priests pray the Liturgy of the Hours, and in some churches other people join the priests for the prayers. But I didn't know any Catholic priests in Los Angeles. This information wouldn't help me find a place to pray in community. Fran didn't intend to be unhelpful. What he took so completely for granted was not instinctively understandable to me. After he entered the Dominican novitiate, however, my connection to him eventually led me to priests I would pray with twice every weekday.

I planned to visit my family in the Bay Area for Thanksgiving and hoped I could join Brother Emmanuel's community for a prayer service. But I realized that I couldn't remember the address of the church that housed the Dominican novitiate, nor could I recall their prayer times. I went to the church's website, and it occured to me that I could find more general information about Dominicans on the internet. So, following a few links from the church's website to one that recruits men to join the order, I discovered a great deal about a novice's formation process.

An introduction to life in the Dominican order is incomplete if the novices remain in only one location. Alongside the elements of novice life I knew of—prayer, community life, introductory classes,

ORDERS ON THE NET

If you know where to look, the internet has a great deal of information about orders. My own searching was haphazard, beginning with my friend Jessica emailing me links to websites of orders she was considering. At that point, reading orders' websites was merely a fun way for me to share in her journey of exploring becoming a nun. Then as I began looking for information about Dominicans, I stumbled across a number of sites that varied significantly in quality and depth. I've put together a website (www.flirtingwithmonasticism.org) that can assist you in your own internet searching.

some ministry activity—I learned that novices were expected to see the various places where Dominicans live and work. During the novitiate they travel down and up the West Coast, visiting various Dominican communities in their province. They maintain their daily rhythms on the road, and sometimes praying Liturgy of the Hours means chanting with their prayer books while riding in their van. Some novices get carsick.

As I read through reflections written by previous novice groups about these tours, I was startled to see references to my own tiny Los Angeles neighborhood. In four years of living there I had never particularly noticed the Catholic church, much less been aware that it's staffed by a whole community of Dominican friars. I searched the internet for information about the church in my neighborhood and confirmed that anyone was welcome to join the friars Monday through Friday in Morning and Evening Prayer. I decided to go the next day, but later that afternoon I wondered, *Why wait until tomorrow? Evening prayer will be happening in two hours!*

How ironic that for several years of truly desiring to be close to a community that prays Liturgy of the Hours, I had not figured out that it could be found a mile down the street from my house.

DAILY PRAYER SERVICES

The Dominican church in Los Angeles practiced a much less elaborate prayer service than what I had experienced at the abbey. Morning and Evening Prayer were each less than fifteen minutes. Lacking any instrumental accompaniment, the only musical element of the prayer time is an a cappella hymn. Every other component is recited as the praying community kneels, stands, bows and sits. In this recitation, however, there is a whole other beauty of rhythm and awareness of community—in some ways more challenging than praying with chant tones.

While this praying community doesn't have separate seating for those in the order, it became obvious that most everyone has a place where they always sit. To follow along with the prayers I would sit next to other women who shared their prayer book with me. Eventually I ordered my own book online.

As the weeks went by I wondered if I could get some sort of teaching on or explanation of Liturgy of the Hours. Though I never found a "how to" class, over several months I eventually learned more. These kinds of prayers have been central for many believers throughout the centuries. Praying by the recitation of psalms is an even older practice from Judaism; Jesus of Nazareth would have regularly prayed in this manner. Today, a diverse spectrum of Christian communities regularly pray at fixed hours, making use of Scripture and other liturgical resources.

Of all the gatherings I have been a part of, no two communities have ever prayed Liturgy of the Hours in exactly the same way. There are a number of possibilities as to what prayer book will be used and how the liturgy will be formed. Each community then makes decisions about music and body postures. An entire service can be chanted and accompanied by music, or have none at all. At Brother Emmanuel's church in San Francisco, for example, the prayer services include numerous chant tones, a distinctive of the Dominican order, whereas the Dominican church in Los Angeles has none. It's rare for a prayer service to occur in only one body posture, lacking any gestures. Moving through several postures, along with gestures such as the sign of the cross, aids the rhythm of the prayer and incorporates more of one's entire being into the prayer.

Generally, once a community establishes how it will pray together, the form is rarely consciously discussed. Newcomers to a community are expected to learn primarily by observation, rather than explicit instructions, how to join the rhythms. Yet there are basic patterns found in praying the hours:

- A service opens with a familiar call to prayer, followed by a hymn or other song sung by everyone.

- Next are selected psalms and possibly other poetic texts from Scripture that the community voices together.

- Then one person reads a selection from Scripture. What follows can vary, but there is often silence to reflect on the Scripture or a response with brief phrases.

- Depending on the prayer service, other elements included at this point are voiced as a community another poetic Scripture text, or possibly a time of intercessory prayer concluding with the Lord's Prayer.

• Every service closes with a brief prayer and often a blessing.

Each prayer service at the different hours of the day has its own variations, depending on the specific purposes of the particular prayer time. For example, a prayer service may feature a time for intercession, a reading of extended selections of Scripture and other devotional materials, a break in the middle of one's workday, an examination of conscience, or a preparation for going to sleep.

The number of times a community gathers throughout each day, and the length of each service, has fluctuated throughout Christian history. Today the most common number of prayer times is five. Sometimes two or more of the prayer times are combined, or a community may decide to allow one or more of the prayer times to be done individually.

Central to the concept of praying the divine office is that whenever and wherever the prayer service takes place, it is to be a shared public prayer. But many who are not a regular part of a prayer community also incorporate Liturgy of the Hours into their own personal prayer practices. As one novice colorfully pointed out to me, "It's public prayer even if you are praying the divine office alone while you are sitting on the toilet."

The moments that have had the greatest impact on me during the Liturgy of the Hours are extended times of personal petitions, typically offered between recited intercessions and the Lord's Prayer. Closing my eyes at this point in a prayer service I can almost forget where I am. I could be at any number of intercessory prayer meetings that I have participated in over the years. Being in a Catholic church, praying with men in white habits, feels similar to being in Steve's dorm room on Thursday night.

CAMPUS PRAYER SERVICES

Sitting across from one another on the first day of my senior year in college, Steve and I tried to build a connection. We tried to like each other. We tried to talk together. And it was not happening.

I knew that prayer was a good thing from participating in numerous prayer gatherings throughout my high school years, even serving as a prayer group leader in Sunday morning youth group. So during my first two years at college I joined in whenever people were meeting to pray. For a time this was every weekday morning at 8:00 a.m.; in another season it was nightly at midnight. I had been amazed by how often people in the Christian fellowship met for prayer and all that they would pray about. Especially new to me was all the prayer that simply was a part of hanging out with Christian friends.

Having studied abroad my entire junior year, I returned to school for my senior year and was introduced to Steve, a sophomore. Though we both had significant friendships with Christians in other parts of the expansive campus, he and I would be the only Christian fellowship leaders living in our part of the campus. Others in the Christian fellowship had been excited for us to meet, but it became rapidly apparent that aside from a shared commitment to Christ, nothing would naturally incline us to spend time together. Our initial difficult meeting came to a close with prayer, and we went our separate ways.

The very next night, watching the new female freshman in my hall going out to party, I was heartbroken, and driven to find someone to join me in praying for the women. Vaguely remembering the location of Steve's dorm room, I went there and found Steve. I walked in, told him I needed to pray, closed the door and burst into tears.

The need was so apparent and urgent that we entered into a time of extended intercessory prayer after only the briefest explanation. Over the next few days, while we never crossed paths in our daily routines on the small campus, we somehow found ourselves led to pray together at night for our college community. We decided to commit to praying together at 10:00 p.m. every Sunday through Thursday.

As the weeks went by we never did see each other during the day. We had different majors, different groups of friends and different places where we each hung out. We weren't trying to become friends, and talking to each other wasn't becoming easier. I knew he was on the campus because he would turn up for prayer. When we met we would share the prayer needs and concerns that were on our heart, perhaps sing a song or read a portion of Scripture, and spend the majority of the hour petitioning God with our intercessions. When our prayer times wrapped up, Steve and I would go our separate ways.

Three months passed of us praying, and it dawned on us one night that a connection was growing between us. We were surprised that God was doing something in our midst, unifying us in spite of our failure to instinctively relate to one another. Returning together after being apart for several weeks of the winter break, Steve and I found that we had missed each other. We began to build a friendship in the second half of the school year around our commitment to pray together.

A benefit of our having such divergent personalities and different maturity levels was that, for all the intimacy in our ministry partnership, neither of us was romantically attracted to the other. What formed instead was a real closeness, a sense of being children of the same heavenly Father. As I had been mentored by older brothers and sisters in Christ during my first two years of college, now I was mentoring this precious younger brother. Today, nearly a decade and many life adventures later, we still share a sense of siblinghood.

The time of intercessory prayer during Morning and Evening Prayer at the Dominican church in San Francisco is reminiscent of my experience with Steve and really any number of other intercessory prayer meetings. The chief difference is this: in Liturgy of the Hours, intercessory prayer is surrounded by the rich support of much chanted and recited Scripture. The intensity of intercessory prayer combined with the structure of Liturgy of the Hours results in an extraordinary way of being with God.

THANKSGIVING

After a few days of joining the friars in Los Angeles for Morning and Evening Prayer, I left to spend Thanksgiving with my family in the

Bay Area. On Friday morning I drove to the Dominican church in San Francisco. With confidence in having more of a sense of the prayer services, instead of sitting and watching Morning Prayer and the Office of Readings, I sat with the praying community at the front of the sanctuary, next to other women who were seated there. Before the service started everyone was silently preparing, and Brother Emmanuel acknowledged me with a friendly, welcoming glance. At the end of the prayers he made his way over to me, saying, "Happy Thanksgiving! How are you doing?" It took me a few excited attempts before I could coherently explain my recent discovery that the Dominican church in Los Angeles was very close to my home, and I could now regularly join a community to pray Liturgy of the Hours.

He then asked me if I was learning the Dominican chant tones.

As a novice, he was in the process of learning them. Of the several forms of prayer central to a Dominican novice's formation, Liturgy of the Hours is the most complicated, in part because it requires musical skill. During their novitiate and seminary years, the Dominican brothers do a ton of chanting. Novices even attend music classes to strengthen them in leading the singing and chanting during services. Though not everyone in orders is musically gifted, I did observe all the novices noticeably improving over time.

Chanting Liturgy of the Hours is frequently mentioned by men exploring orders as one of the main factors that specifically drew them to the Dominicans. Stories are told of the founder of the order, Dominic, feeling strongly that the success of the friars' ministry would be directly connected to the strength of their prayer life. He would walk around as the original community of friars prayed the divine office, exhorting the friars to chant more bravely. Dominic believed that apart from faithful prayer, hours of study and preparation would not amount to anything of lasting significance.

Sadly, with the many pressures upon those in full-time ministry, and the limitations of musical ability of others who join the friars in the prayer times, chanting tends to fall by the wayside in many communities. When I told Brother Emmanuel that the Dominican community in Los Angeles does not chant he immediately said, "You can encourage them to do so." His response underscored just how much he didn't grasp what an outsider I am to the Dominican world, that his suggestion was preposterous. Not only was I merely a new participant in the church's Liturgy of the Hours, I was new to this style of prayer. I was only at the beginning of learning about Dominicans; it wasn't my place to have any attitude other than being a respectful newcomer among their communities.

A YOUNG MONK'S FAMILY

During my first visit to the abbey near San Diego with Jen, several novices
made their first vows. Most of the men in the monastic community—
even two of the novices—appeared to be fifteen to twenty years older than I,
but one novice was near my age. Jen and I were sitting
right behind his family. It seemed as though his brothers couldn't
fathom what he was doing. We overheard them whisper,
"He's crazy" and "He has no idea what he's missing out on."

It is actually very common for family members to be confused,
if not hostile, about a person's decision to enter an order. Even families
who are very involved in their church are often initially unsupportive of their
daughter or son becoming a priest, friar, monk, sister or nun.

This reaction is usually about fearing the unknown. Families expect their
children to grow up, get married and have children.
Joining an order is not what they expected, and the change can feel
sudden, dramatic. Over time, as family and friends learn more about the
community and that joining an order is an ongoing process
involving several years of decision-making, most become supportive.

Whether or not that young monk's brothers understand what he is doing,
in my visits to the abbey I see him praying and working as a
member of that community. Though I have never even said hello to
him, his stable presence in the years following his first profession
is a reminder: though he has chosen to not have children,
n the Benedictine community he has gained many, many brothers.

LOVE?

Responding to my puzzled expression, Brother Emmanuel shifted the conversation, asking me how my visit with my family was going. Suddenly I was conscious that while I took for granted spending Thanksgiving with my family, the men in the novitiate had given this up. I wondered, had the night before been a sad time for them? In the bustle of people moving around us, I didn't ask this question.

I gathered that our conversation needed to be wrapped up soon. But he lowered his voice and said, "I've been meaning to write you." I couldn't bring myself to look in his eyes as I responded. "I have so not stressed about that. You are in a different world here. Whatever is needed for this world, that's what you need to do."

Brother Emmanuel appeared comforted by what I said, but then sad. "I'll send something to you," he said. Then after a quick hug, I watched him disappear into the priory. Saddened by only having a few minutes to interact with him, rather than a longer conversation like my previous visits, I hoped we would have more time together when I returned to San Francisco for Christmas.

Back in Los Angeles, a friend teasingly mentioned her husband's reaction when he heard that I was regularly getting up early in order to pray Liturgy of the Hours with a community of Dominican friars: "Wow, Karen must really be in love with that guy."

I thought that over a bit. "Sure I like the guy. But there is no way any man, no matter how thoughtful or intelligent or attractive, would cause me to willingly give up sleep morning after morning." Getting out of bed is not easy for me. Love was getting me up in the morning for prayer, but it was a much deeper love.

I did hope, though, that Brother Emmanuel would write me. Toward the end of October I had sent him a long letter, but I hadn't received a reply. I assumed he either couldn't or didn't want to communicate with me. But after his comment at Thanksgiving, I was now hopefully expectant about hearing from him.

In the meantime, I became a regular presence at the Dominican church in Los Angeles. A smiling grandmother stopped me one evening as I was walking out of the church after prayer. "Are you a lady?" she asked.

Uh, what? Last time I checked I was female. This woman must be asking something other than the obvious answer to her question. But what did she mean?

Not getting any response, the woman rephrased her question. "Are you a Dominican Sister?"

"Oh, no," I told her. "I just love praying Liturgy of the Hours." Then, deciding to reveal more, I leaned in and quietly confessed, "I'm a Presbyterian pastor."

She looked stunned, puzzled. But she collected herself, smiled and said, "We are the same."

I returned her smile, but I wasn't sure what else to say. This whole situation of being around a Dominican community was unusual. And it was getting more unusual, as another spiritual practice held every Friday was becoming meaningful to me: eucharistic adoration.

4

IN THE PRESENCE OF CHRIST

Participating in Adoration & the Eucharist

The Dominican life, from the beginning, is a journey filled with prayer. The novices' lives are intentionally structured to protect them from frantic busyness, and to deepen the intimacy of their relationship with Jesus. In addition to gathering several times a day for praying Liturgy of the Hours as a community, the novices have an hour every day of silent individual prayer during eucharistic adoration.

ADORATION IN SAN FRANCISCO

Though I frequently went to adoration at the Dominican church in my neighborhood, only once near the end of my year visiting the novices did I end up sharing in an hour of adoration with them. Walking into the huge church in San Francisco that Sunday evening, it dawned on me that I did not know where adoration would be held. Brother Emmanuel was at the front of the sanctuary, so I went to say hello and ask him where I should sit. He appeared to be confused by that question—he'd been  doing this every day for nine months—but eventually he motioned with his hand and said, "Just sit anywhere out there."

CONFUSING QUESTIONS

Throughout my year exploring various aspects of Dominican life,
it was common for friars to be stumped or to give unclear answers
to what I assumed were easy questions.

Being a Domican and doing what Dominicans do is not merely
their everyday journey. Though this is an unusual and
spiritually fulfilling way to live, Dominicans are generally
unaccustomed to explaining the rhythms of their lives to others.

Following adoration, Brother Emmanuel realized my confusion
and went out of his way to give me the prayer book and other directions
needed for participating in Night Prayer. When several additional prayers
were said, he made sure that I found the right page to follow along.

"Out there" was a large space. I found a seat in an empty pew near the front where a few others were sitting.

Soon the small service began. The novice with the strongest singing voice led us in a Latin hymn while a priest brought out a con-

secrated host and prepared it for adoration. As it is generally done, the priest placed the consecrated host in an ornate golden holder, called a monstrance (from a Latin word meaning "to show" or "to reveal"). Almost always, the design of a monstrance will include a sunburst, with the rays emanating out in a circle around the consecrated host.

With the monstrance as a focal point, the gathered community entered into a time of silent reflection. Some were sitting, others kneeling, and when I looked over to where Brother Emmanuel was, I saw him sitting cross-legged on the ground as he wrote in his journal. Returning my attention to the front of the church, I felt internally prompted to kneel. As I knelt on the kneeler, I found myself repeating in my entire being for some minutes, "Holy. Holy. Holy." In the intensity of this time I knew something spiritually profound was happening, even as I cannot rationally explain why. When I returned to sitting, I continued to pray, did some reflective writing and read from my Bible.

After an hour of silence, the time of adoration was brought to a close. The novices assisted the priest with the brief liturgy, beginning with a Latin hymn and a short prayer recited by the priest. Then the priest put on a humeral veil, a long strip of fabric similar to a very wide stole, using it to cover his hands while he picked up and moved the monstrance in blessing over those present. The fabric between the priest's hands and the monstrance is a symbolic expression that Jesus, rather than the priest, is actually giving the blessing.

The priest then returned to kneeling before the monstrance and led the congregation in a litany called the Divine Praises. One Dominican priest suggested to me that saying them can be viewed as counteracting all the times God's name is spoken in cursing: "Blessed be God. Blessed be his Holy Name. Blessed be Jesus Christ, true God and true man . . . "

After the Divine Praises the priest removed the consecrated host from the monstrance, and we all stood for a closing song.

Often during a liturgy of eucharistic adoration incense is used to create a delightful smell and the beautiful sight of rising smoke in the church. The lingering sweet smell on Fridays at the church in Los An-

geles would tell me that adoration had ended just before I showed up for Evening Prayer. So whenever possible I would leave work early on Fridays to have time in adoration.

EXPLAINING ADORATION

Eucharistic adoration involves a wafer of bread, consecrated through a liturgy of the Eucharist during mass, being exposed for a period of time in the presence of prayerful worshipers. Ordinarily consecrated hosts that remain after a mass are kept locked up in a special ornate

container, called a tabernacle. Catholic churches generally have the tabernacle at the very front of the church or in a special side chapel near the front. Worshipers then pray in the presence of the Eucharist. Many Catholics genuflect before the tabernacle, lowering their right knee to the ground as a sign of devotion. I heard a woman teaching a small child to genuflect as they were leaving the church: "Say goodbye to Jesus."

Catholics practice extraordinary care for the consecrated host, often referred to as the Blessed Sacrament, because of their belief in the actual presence of Christ's body and blood in the Eucharist: after consecration the bread and wine retain the appearance of bread and wine, but the elements have actually, substantially, transformed into the body and blood of Christ. In the Eucharist, then, is the physical presence of Jesus.

Spending time in adoration often draws participants deeper into a life of prayer. While group worship experiences are permissible during adoration, individual prayer is much more common. It is usually appropriate during adoration to read Scripture or other devotional writings, to do personal writing or anything you would do during an intimate time with a close friend.

It is moving to consider how much time Dominic, the founder of the Dominican order, spent in intimate prayer with Christ. It was his custom to sleep on the floor of the churches he visited when preaching, but many nights he would stay up for long periods of time praying before the tabernacle. His companions would have their sleep disrupted when Dominic's private prayers led him to tearful sobbing and groaning. As recounted by Dominic's companions, his most frequent prayer was that he would be given a true love for those who did not yet know Christ, that he would give his life in the ministry of drawing people to Christ, as ultimately in crucifixion Christ had given his life for others. In his prayers Dominic incorporated his entire body, standing, kneeling, bowing and often repeatedly prostrating himself in the presence of the Eucharist.

BEING WITH JESUS

The sermons at the church where I grew up frequently highlighted the importance of spending time with Jesus in prayer. And what made the greatest impression on me was a tract I was given the summer before my freshman year of high school. At the end of a week of Christian summer camp, my cabin counselor sent me home with *My Heart—Christ's Home* by Robert Boyd Munger. As I read the narrator's journey with Jesus through various rooms of her heart, what resonated loudest was the discussion of being with Jesus in the living room.

Munger describes the living room of the heart as a quiet, intimate and aesthetically pleasing space. What is particularly evocative is the image of Jesus faithfully waiting to meet with me for a delightful time together. Far too often I allow myself to become busy and distracted doing many things, but Jesus is there, still waiting. As Munger reminds me, only one thing is truly needed:

> The truth that Christ desires my companionship, that He wants
> me to be with Him and waits for me, has done more to trans-
> form my quiet time with God than any other single fact. Don't
> let Christ wait alone in the living room of your heart, but every
> day find time when, with your Bible and in prayer, you may be
> together with Him.

For all that my church taught me, I can't think of any structure
through which the church regularly created intentional spaces to actually be with Jesus. Experiences of adoration in Catholic communities, by contrast, have been a wonderful blessing in drawing me into
the living room of my heart. Does the visible presence of the Blessed
Sacrament actually mean that Jesus is more present and available
than other times in our days? I don't know. What I do know is that
the structure of this practice enables me to be much more present to,
and focused on, our Lord.

Sometimes this means a deep peaceful stillness, at other times a tan-
gible sense of the Holy Spirit. While thinking about the content of this
book, I found it particularly helpful to bring a notepad to adoration
and write up ideas. One lengthy, quiet New Year's Day afternoon at adoration in Los Angeles, I was finally able to make space for a book I had
been wanting for months to read, Henri Nouwen's reflections on icons
Behold the Beauty of the Lord. Similar to other very worshipful experiences, the context of adoration enabled me to be intentional about
more deeply entering into a particular awareness of God's presence.

Dominican friars who have finished the novitiate aren't required to
maintain a daily hour of adoration. From what I've observed, however, it remains an important source of spiritual sustenance for many
Dominicans.

BLESSING AT MASS

Adoration is understood as both an extension of mass and something that leads people to more frequent participation in mass. Mass is the pinnacle of Catholic worship, with a liturgy of the Word followed by a liturgy of the Eucharist. It amazes me how often worship services take place in Catholic churches. Dominican novices are at mass every day. At the Dominican church in Los  Angeles mass is held twice a day, with six masses on Sunday. Far beyond only Sunday morning gatherings, Catholic churches provide opportunities for corporate worship every day. Thus, throughout my year of praying with Dominicans, I wound up attending mass at least several times a month.

Participation in mass (or adoration, or Liturgy of the Hours) does not make one Catholic. In the liturgy of the Eucharist, the divergence between Catholics and everyone else becomes most apparent. Only reconciled Catholics are to receive the Eucharist, Christ's body and blood. Even as I experience so many beautiful moments of shared worship with Catholics, the Eucharist is a reminder that Christian unity is not yet fully realized.

When people at mass are invited to come forward to receive the Eucharist I join the line. But instead of putting my arms out to receive a consecrated host, I cross my arms on my chest to indicate that I am to receive a blessing. This is one part of mass that is not predictable. For a church service in which things are so prescribed, it's surprising to discover the incredible variety in the experience of receiving a blessing. Anyone assisting in serving the Eucharist—from archbishop to lay minister—can offer the blessing, and they can choose to do any number of things. Most often the person will move the Blessed Sacrament in the sign of a cross and say a very brief triune blessing: "May God bless you in the name of the Father, the Son and the Holy Spirit." Some will put down the consecrated host with an impressive efficiency of movement, and then reach out their hand to the recipient's forehead while saying a blessing.

Sometimes the process of receiving a blessing can feel perfunctory. Once I had to tell a visiting Dominican priest three times that I was not to receive the Eucharist before he finally offered a distracted blessing. Yet more often than not, in that moment I shiver with a sense of Christ's nearness. The most memorable time was a mid-week evening mass at the cathedral in Denver where, holding the consecrated host in front of me, the server uniquely said, "Receive Jesus in your heart." Something about this just clicked. I felt nothing lacking in my experience of the Eucharist as I was truly invited to receive Jesus.

Aside from the moments of the Eucharist where I would experience separation from Catholics, however, I did learn to participate in the rhythms of mass with everyone else. I was honored when a friend of a friend sitting near me during a mass remarked, "Wow, you know the mass better than most Catholics."

REFLECTIONS ON MASS

For all the masses I have attended, it can still be a disorienting experience. As much as I dearly love liturgical experiences, when it comes to the church in worship, I am most at home in simple services with some combination of singing, praying and preaching. Liturgical services of mainline denominations, particularly Episcopal and Lutheran churches, have inherited their format from the Roman Catholic mass, but these churches almost always provide a handout to facilitate entering into the service. I have yet to visit a Catholic church that proactively helps outsiders to follow along with what is taking place. It's generally assumed that everyone at mass knows the entire liturgy from a lifetime of participating in mass. Anyone else, it's assumed, will learn quickly, for aside from which passages of Scripture are read and the content of the homily, there is very little variation in a Roman Catholic mass.

Even the Scripture reading, however, feels awkward to me. In mass, the emphasis is on hearing the passages as they are read, rather than on reading the passage. Rarely have the Catholic churches I've visited had Bibles in the pews. Nor have Scripture readers told the congregation the chapters and verses of what is being read, and paused for people to find the passage in their Bible so they could read along. Even though I am gaining an appreciation for the practice of hearing Scripture, sometimes I do take out my Bible to follow along, such as the Easter Vigil Mass. Hearing the lengthy Easter story told through several extended readings of Scripture passages was a joy; it was far more Scripture then I had ever previously experienced in an Easter service.

Over and over, Catholics have told me how receiving Jesus in the Eucharist forms the center of their faith life. This can easily be seen in the care and reverence that clergy and eucharistic ministers have in handling the elements of the Lord's Supper. A ministry that novices frequently assist with is bringing the Eucharist to those whose circumstances prevent them from being at mass. One elderly woman in a nursing home, Mildred, has been regularly visited by many years of novices in another province. Each year of novices has inherited a custom of bringing not only the Eucharist to Mildred, but also hamburgers. Mildred would say that it's the Eucharist she most appreciates, but novices have learned that it's best to always stop at White Castle on their way to visit her.

For novices who go on to prepare for the Roman Catholic priesthood, a possibility for only unmarried males, there is an anticipation of someday leading the celebration of mass. As one Dominican priest told me (mostly) in jest, "I'd be married if it weren't for the Eucharist. It's the Eucharist that keeps me in the Roman Catholic church."

A college roommate who had since joined the Catholic church told me about feeling drawn toward becoming a clergyperson. I asked if she would consider being ordained in the Episcopal church, which has a very similar liturgy to the Catholic church and ordains women to the priesthood. She considered this and responded, "I don't think I can let go of the Catholic understanding of the Eucharist," she said. "It's too important to me." Because of this commitment, it is likely my friend won't ever become a clergyperson.

COMMUNION ON CAMPUS

In sharp contrast to the Dominicans, my college Christian fellowship group didn't place much emphasis on attending church, nor celebrating Communion. Where people chose to attend Sunday morning worship services was the one part of our group's spiritual life that we didn't share in common. And it was somewhat acceptable to not attend any church service. While those with cars were always glad to offer transportation to the church service they attended, there wasn't expectation or accountability.

Feeling well rooted in my home church hundreds of miles away, I viewed Sunday morning in my college years as an opportunity to explore the incredible variety of how God's people worship. Whenever I found out that a classmate attended church, I would ask to go with them. Eating brunch together in the cafeteria after the service, we would then talk about the opportunities for Christian fellowship on campus.

Our group had a Sunday evening gathering once a month with another Christian fellowship. It was almost a formal worship service, usually including a "rip and dip" Communion celebration by intinction. We would process in a line to rip a piece of bread from a common loaf. We would then dip the piece of bread into a large communal cup filled with wine, then return to our seats for a time of meditation. This form of Communion  was strange at first; my home church had always passed trays of bread and cups of grape juice for everyone to receive while sitting in prayerful meditation.

None of these differences were particularly disturbing to me, since the process for Communion was always carefully explained. But it would be a decade before I would understand how difficult it must have been for my Catholic friends in the fellowship to participate in these Communion services.

After celebrating Maundy Thursday, Good Friday and Easter Vigil/Easter Sunday (the full Easter Triduum) at the Dominican church in Los Angeles, I went on retreat with a diverse group of evangelicals. The closing session of the retreat took place at a Catholic monastery and included a Communion celebration. Communion felt remarkably similar to our fellowship group's celebrations ten years prior—the person who coordinated the logistics for the service had been involved in a similar campus group. The difference was our speaker, an evangelical who has spent a great deal of time with Catholics. The large loaf of leavened bread—typical for evangelical services but uncommon in a Catholic context—startled him. "Wow, this sure isn't a Catholic group," he said, encouraging us to take large pieces.

After the service, I sat and stared at the sizable remaining portion of the bread sitting on the table. In the churches I grew up in, the left-over bread is not reserved as a focus of adoration. I knew this bread would either be eaten without reverence or just thrown away. A light went off in my head. I thought about watching people in my church clean up after a Communion service and what I had seen of Catholics cleaning up after mass. How Communion elements are handled depends on how we understand what's taking place when we hear, "This is my body . . . this cup is the new covenant in my blood . . . do this in remembrance of me."

OBEDIENCE AND FREEDOM

I talked with a Catholic Sister about how she has sorted out different approaches to Communion. She didn't have any easily reached conclusions. Working in an ecumenical setting that offers both Catholic and Anglican worship services, she described the tension of Christian freedom and respect for the authority of the Catholic Church's teachings. She receives the Eucharist from the Catholic priest, but finds it painful to hold back from participating fully with the community in the Anglican service, led by a female Anglican priest who has been an important pastor in the Sister's life.

Even as I find spiritual sustenance in many different Communion celebrations, I recognize with great sadness that Christian unity will likely not be found in the Lord's Supper. On a pragmatic level, a needless stumbling block between Christian communities could be smoothed out by, as the retreat speaker suggested, trying not to have lots of bread and wine left over at the conclusion of Communion. I don't know that these divergent views of Communion must be reconciled, however, particularly if somehow I can be welcomed to join in wherever the Lord's Supper is shared. At the end of our conversation, the Sister pointed out, "If you actually stop and think about the original event—Jesus sharing a meal with his followers—it really was quite a simple thing."

O SACRED BANQUET

A nine-year-old friend of mine, David, reminded me how confusing communion can be when he interrupted a Seder meal and held up a piece of matzo bread that was being used to celebrate communion. "If this is bread, how can this be Jesus' body?" he loudly asked. All the theologically trained adults sitting around the child looked at him in awed silence. Unknowingly, he had stumbled upon this unresolved theological debate in the church. Having been David's Sunday school teacher, I know he would have liked a definitive answer. Thankfully, none of the adults rushed in with a neatly packaged response. Instead David was affirmed for his thoughtful question.

While churches generally have systematic theologies that attempt to answer this question—my tradition, for example, understands the Lord's Supper as an experience within a worshiping community of the real spiritual presence of Jesus somehow in real bread and wine—how often does our focus on maintaining the "correct" theological understanding fully explain these sacred moments? What is God more excited about: our perfect understanding or our relationship with Jesus? When David gets older I hope he has the opportunity to learn more about the debates around Communion issues. However, the far greater desire in my heart is that David will be close to Jesus all the days of his life.

Much of the Communion event is really a mystery. Sometimes I tell Dominican friends, "It's not that I don't believe what you believe about the Eucharist. It's that I believe it less fervently, remaining in wonderment about the mystery." Thomas Aquinas, a formidable Dominican scholar of the thirteenth century, composed a prayer frequently recited by the Dominicans about the Eucharist. I've prayed it countless times in my year of praying with Dominican communities, and it's become one of my favorite prayers:

> O Sacred Banquet, in which Christ becomes our food,
> the memory of His passion is celebrated,
> the soul is filled with grace
> and a pledge of future glory is given to us.
> You gave them bread from heaven, containing every blessing.
> O God, in this wonderful Sacrament You have left us a
>   memorial of Your passion.
> Help us, we beg You, so to reverence the sacred mysteries
>   of Your Body and Blood
> that we may constantly feel in our lives the effects of Your
>   redemption,
> Who live and reign forever. Amen.

CHRISTMAS MASS IN SAN FRANCISCO

The most beautiful experience of mass throughout my first year with

the Dominicans was a midnight service on Christmas Eve. In earlier visits to the Dominican church in San Francisco, the gothic architecture and elaborate art was more than I could take in. But in the dark of night, this church with many candles glowing was hauntingly beautiful. Beginning with an hour of singing Christmas carols, the songs and melodies of Christmas were woven throughout the service. The friars processed in to "O Come, All Ye Faithful." Yet Brother Emmanuel was not among them.

Two days earlier I had stopped by the church for Evening Prayer. After prayer some novices told me that many of those in the priory had been ill. Brother Emmanuel was so sick that he couldn't get out of bed. When he didn't process in with the friars at the Christmas Eve mass, I knew I wouldn't get to talk with him during this visit to the Bay area. Inside, I was torn between sympathy and disappointment. No correspondence had come from him in the weeks between Thanksgiving and Christmas, and now I wouldn't even get to talk with him.

At the end of the midnight mass, I chatted with the other novices and gave them a Christmas card with a few lines of well wishes for their holiday celebration, then drove away from the church. Mass had prepared me for Christmas, but I was sad to return home to Los Angeles a few days later. Tears leaked out of my eyes as I told friends what had—or really what hadn't—happened over the Christmas holiday.

> Me: "I just don't know what to think or feel. I have no more clarity about this situation after visiting his priory twice during Christmas. The more time that goes by without hearing from him, the more I'm afraid to hope for the possibility of being in a relationship with him. If I continue to hope, it makes me vulnerable to being hurt by him."

> Them: "Oh Karen, I'm so sorry for you. What are you going to do?"

Me: "Until I talk directly with Brother Emmanuel, I'm not quite ready to let go. I'll just have to wait. And I'm starting to get the sense that God has something bigger than relating to Brother Emmanuel in all of this for me."

Them: "What do you mean?"

Me: "Well, the more I'm learning about the Dominican order—even the practices that are difficult to understand—the more it's blessing my spiritual journey. Going to the Christmas Eve mass was incredible. And a few weeks ago while I was praying, I sensed a calling to continue to learn about the Dominicans and the Catholic church—perhaps come to love them."

I was drawn to love the Dominican world, and even to immerse myself in it. I discovered that would mean encountering Mary.

5

ENCOUNTERING MARY

Saying the Rosary

*G*rowing up in the evangelical world, I knew Mary, the mother of Jesus, as merely an accessory at Christmas time. Every birth story requires a pregnant woman. Any further references to Mary as a presence in Jesus' life on earth were largely ignored. Somehow the mentions in Scripture of Mary at key events, such as the crucifixion and Pentecost, never entered my consciousness.

Needless to say, it's hard for someone like me to know how to respond to the pervasive presence of Mary in Catholic art, prayers and teaching. In Los Angeles, a familiar depiction of Mary is the Virgin of Guadalupe. The origin of this image comes from the story of Mary appearing in 1531 to an indigenous Mexican peasant, having the same dark skin tone as him and speaking with him in his own language. As the story spread, many indigenous Mexicans became a part of the Catholic Church, and today the Virgin of Guadalupe is a central figure for Catholics from that area. Portray-  als of the Virgin of Guadalupe can be spotted in Los Angeles on almost anything, including tee-shirts, night lights and window decals.

The summer after my freshman year of college—long before I had even heard of Dominicans—I visited ancient Christian communities in Palestine and saw many depictions of Mary holding Jesus. This was a very different Mary from the Virgin of Guadalupe. The expres-sion on her face looked gloomy to me. Reading up on Eastern Orthodox icons I discovered that this image of Mary is understood to express tenderness and patience.

However, upon entering the Catholic church in the Palestinian village of Beir Ziet, where I would spend much of the summer, I was shocked to see an enormous mosaic of the Virgin of Guadalupe. Why this image, rather than one of the images of Mary commonly found in the Middle East? And how did this mosaic of Mary end up so far away from the Western Hemisphere?

It turns out that a leader in the Catholic Church from Latin America had visited the Jerusalem area with the hope of building a church in honor of the Virgin of Guadalupe. At that time the church in Beir Zeit was praying for the funds to finish building its half-completed structure. The result is surely the only Our Lady of Guadalupe Catholic Church in the Middle East. Throughout the entire church are gorgeous mosaics from Latin America donated by the benefactor.

Being so far from home that summer, I was unexpectedly comforted by the mosaics. They also underscored just how internationally connected the Catholic church is.

PRAYING FOR MARY'S INTERCESSION

Mary is not just present in the church through iconography. Mary is also a part of many Catholics' prayer life. Usually this does not involve praying *to* Mary but rather asking *for* Mary's prayers of intercession—somewhat similar to asking a friend or trusted spiritual leader to pray for you or prayer concerns on your heart.

SHARING CHRISTIAN FAITH

*With my first in-depth introduction to the Catholic church occurring
in the Middle East, the setting reinforced our unity as Christians.
Christians there of any branch of the church are a very small minority
among a Muslim majority. Though Christianity began in the region,
and has had a continuous presence as a result of the region's
ancient Orthodox churches, it is often a struggle to be Christian.*

*Given the effort required merely to survive as a Christian,
much less theological squabbling occurs when compared with places
where Christianity is flourishing and powerful. In light of the urgent
need for support in vibrantly living out our Christian faith,
sharing the same Scriptures and following the same triune God
was enough to bring us together. Departing from the Middle East
at the end of the summer, I had gained a love for much more of the
body of Christ, recognizing that Christian unity can be
a matter of context and perspective.*

Asking Mary to "pray for us" is most commonly done in the practice of saying the rosary. Formalized during the sixteenth century in Europe, the rosary is a series of repetitive prayers that are said with the aid of a loop of beads. Far from being a uniquely Catholic style of prayer, prayer beads have been a common feature for centuries in many of the world's religions. The rosary's structure gave the predominately illiterate population of the faithful, who did not have access to praying a complicated Divine Office, a meaningful way to do liturgical prayer.

The 150 repetitions of the rosary's central prayer—the "Hail Mary"—are seen as corresponding to a monk or nun's praying all 150 of the psalms. Yet, in contrast to the public nature of the Divine Office, the rosary is always a private prayer of personal devotion—even when people gather to pray it together.

More than just a spoken prayer, the rosary is both vocal and mental. At designated spots in the cycle of prayers, space is left to reflect upon various moments in Jesus' life. The Catholic church has designated four sets, called mysteries, of five events each. Eventually as one becomes familiar with the repeated spoken prayers, meditating on the life of Jesus becomes the primary work of the prayer. The rhythm of repetition creates a focus, allowing a person to remain prayerfully centered in Christ for an extended period of time.

In the twentieth century, praying the rosary was especially linked to praying for peace on earth. While living in Palestine, a place greatly in need of peace, I was blessed to get to know members of the Sisters of the Rosary, a community of Sisters founded in Palestine at the end of the nineteenth century. With a large main convent in Jerusalem, these sisters live in small communities scattered throughout Palestine and neighboring areas, teaching in Catholic schools and assisting Catholic priests in parish programs. As their name suggests, a key part of their spiritual life is regularly praying the rosary.

With the pervasive presence of rosaries in the Catholic world, simply having a rosary is not always a good indicator of a person's faithful prayer life. Once while riding in a car a friend had borrowed from his sister, I noticed a rosary wrapped around the rearview mirror. Curious, I pointed to it and asked if his sister had a vibrant faith life. He replied, "Oh no, that has more to do with our ethnic identity. To be [part of our culture] is to hang a rosary from your rearview mirror. Everybody does it. I do pray for her, that she would come to church and actually be praying the rosary."

MARY AND ME

Clearly Mary has a much more prominent role in the spiritual life of Catholics than what I as an evangelical can easily grasp. However, after the summer in Palestine I experienced something I could only describe as an encounter with Mary when I returned to my college campus. Like many who have invigorating crosscultural experiences, I hankered to return to the region as soon as possible. I put a ton of energy into attempting to put together a study abroad/mission service program that would allow me to return to Palestine six months later. As I lined up all the necessary logistical details, I came to the point where I had to commit to the decision to go.

While I had put a great deal of thought into the practical aspects of the decision, I knew I also needed to pray with others for guidance about what to do. A prayerful mentor of mine, Brook, arranged to meet with me. After a brief opening prayer to still our hearts, we sat in silence together for a while to listen to what God might say. I shared first the impressions I had: appreciation for all that I had been learning that fall about loving God and others before myself, the joy I had found in serving the people around me at college. God was growing my desire to see the fruits of the Spirit more fully lived out in my life. They were all peaceful impressions.

Then Brook shared. From the first word he said, "Mary," I was overcome with emotion. As he continued to speak I was increasingly finding myself, atypically, crying loudly—at times wailing. As Brook had been listening in prayer, he had a vision of a very pregnant Mary simply going around her house doing regular, daily tasks. Accompanying this image were the words from Luke 1:46: "My soul doth magnify the Lord." The image was one of peace and expectation.

Later that same night, I went to a large group intercessory prayer meeting that had begun at the start of the semester to pray for revival on our campus. It met at midnight every Sunday through Thursday for the entire semester, and a number of wonderful things had happened on our campus and for me personally. This night a line from the Scripture passage read at the opening of the meeting stood out— Elizabeth's words resonated with me: "Why am I so favored, that the mother of my Lord should come to me?"

I had the sense that somehow Jesus' mother, Mary, was watching over and caring for me. It was all so foreign and strange, overwhelming me to tears. Yet knowing that I was specifically praying about returning to Beir Zeit, I realized that the people there would probably understand better than myself what I had experienced. With their church honoring the Virgin of Guadalupe and Sisters of the Rosary living in their community, it might not seem so strange to them for me to say that an experience of Mary was leading me to stay in the United States.

It was sad and disappointing to not be quickly returning to Palestine, a people and place I remain passionate about. But to be there would be challenging, not peaceful and nurturing. In continuing to pray about this decision the following day, I felt further confirmation that the best place for me during that season was the familiar environment of my college campus. Even with the embarrassment of telling the people who had been helping me with my plans that I decided to not go, I knew that staying at my college was the best thing to do. The following year, after more prayerful discernment, I did return to the Middle East for four amazing months.

DOMINICANS AND THE ROSARY

Since that experience in my sophomore year of college, I've rarely thought about Mary; nothing in my evangelical world brought her to mind. However, with my exploration of the Dominican world, I was once again confronted with Mary and the rosary. Every day at the Dominican church in Los Angeles, Morning Prayer is concluded with an additional prayer that Jesus would, "through the intercession of your most Holy Mother Mary, Virgin Immaculate, and Queen of the Holy Rosary . . . increase the number of friar preachers."

Given my feelings for Brother Emmanuel, I was not always certain I wanted to pray this prayer for more friars. Eventually, though, I decided to join in, for I do believe that an increase in the number of Dominican friars would be a wonderful thing. While reciting the prayer aloud, internally I prayed for help in trusting God with whether or not Brother Emmanuel would be a part of that increase.

What also made me uncertain about the prayer was all the exalted terms for Mary. But around the one line referring to Mary are beautiful lines of prayer, including "following your recommendation to ask the Lord of the Harvest to send laborers to work for the salvation of souls." Looking back on my prayer life, I know that God is very gracious in hearing my heart, even as I say and do foolish things in prayer with good intentions. Though I haven't become comfortable with referring to Mary in this manner, my longing for unity with this faithful community of prayerful Christians is far greater than my need to pass judgment on questionable but nonessential theology.

The most common length for a rosary is five decades—five sets of ten beads—but the rosary worn with a Dominican habit is much longer, with three times the number of beads. Each friar obtained their rosary when they first entered the novitiate, either by making one for themselves or asking to be given one.

DOMINIC'S ROSARY?

Several Dominicans in the history of the order are particularly renowned
for promoting the practice of saying the rosary,
leading to a claim that the rosary was given to Dominic directly
during a vision of Mary. Images of this moment are frequently found in
Dominican churches, yet most Dominicans today will point out
that historical support for this event is pretty slim.
Dominic's earliest biographers don't mention this encounter;
the oldest accounts of this event appear centuries later
in sermons about the rosary.

It's not uncommon for a friar to be unexpectedly yanked when their rosary becomes caught on something. In moving about, the rosary adds a noisy jangle as the beads knock against each other and anything else, particularly when sitting down or standing up. Any attempt for a friar to move quietly is made difficult by these beads. Sometimes I listen for the sound of the beads chattering with each other, and I find it unexpectedly comforting. Mentioning this to a Dominican priest as we heard, but did not yet see, another Dominican approaching, he told me most Dominicans can actually distinguish the particular rosary jangle and footfalls of the others in their community.

Yet the rosary is not just a noisy part of their attire, it is a blessed item that is regularly utilized for prayer.

ME AND THE ROSARY

Even with the general trendiness of prayer beads in popular culture, a

UGH, WHAT IS IT WITH MEN AND SWORDS?

All Dominican friars wear their rosary on their left side as, it is often noted,

a medieval knight would wear his sword.

Putting aside the question of swords and the male psyche,

the explanation of this analogy is that the friar uses the rosary

to engage in the spiritual warfare of prayer.

When struggling with temptation, or other spiritual attack,

it is through saying the rosary that a friar can prevail.

and all the Catholic practices that I was willing to enter into with Dominicans, my boundary was set at saying the rosary. I remained open to someday perhaps using a knotted prayer rope, an implement of the Orthodox church to aid in praying the Jesus Prayer:

Lord Jesus Christ, Son of God,
have mercy on me, a sinner.

I was not interested in learning the prayers of the rosary, nor in following up on invitations to join any of the groups at the Catholic church with whom I could say the rosary. Though the novices said the rosary every day (sometimes together and sometimes on their own) as a practice of personal devotion, it was not anything I ever had the opportunity to join them in doing. But then the novices' tour brought them to the Dominican church in my neighborhood for a week.

I enjoyed experiencing the novices' world during my visits in San Francisco. But back in Los Angeles after Christmas, I also knew I felt really confused about how to relate to Brother Emmanuel. Occasionally seeing him continued to stir up strong feelings in me, and he was

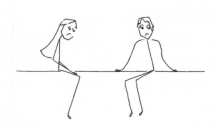

always attentive when interacting with me. Yet otherwise it felt like I kept unexpectedly hitting walls. With the group traveling during the month of January, there was no way I could contact Brother Emmanuel even if I had wanted to do so. All I could do was wait for their tour to arrive in Los Angeles. As best I was I able, I tried not to dwell on the situation and just waited, distracted by an intensive accounting class I was taking every evening after work.

Then on a Tuesday evening as I was rushing in late to Evening Prayer, I noticed there were several more men in white habits than usual. Without consciously thinking about it, I went directly to the pew where Brother Emmanuel was sitting and sat next to him. My heart was racing; it was challenging to focus on the rhythm of the prayers.

All the feelings of attraction and confusion, which I had been ignoring during the previous weeks, came to the surface over the next few days. During this time I had several informative conversations about Dominican life with Brother Emmanuel's fellow novices and their novice master. Yet I became sad as Brother Emmanuel and I were not given the opportunity to talk about the emotions between us.

Early on Thursday morning a strange thing happened. In that state of first waking, when one is still dreaming, I found myself vividly reciting the central prayer of the rosary,

Hail, Mary, full of grace
the Lord is with thee.

SCRIPTURE ADDRESSING MARY

To those who are unfamiliar with the Hail Mary, as I was, the prayer

can seem odd. Yet over half of the words in the short prayer

come directly from the beginning of the Gospel of Luke.

The first sentence in the prayer is drawn from the words of the angel

Gabriel when he tells Mary she will conceive and give birth to Jesus:

"Hail, favored one! The Lord is with you" (Luke 1:28).

The second sentence of the prayer is found a few verses later as Mary's

relative Elizabeth, filled with the Holy Spirit, proclaims,

"Most blessed are you among women, and blessed is the fruit of your

womb" (Luke 1:42). These two pieces of Scripture were

linked together early on as statements of God's favor on Mary.

The third sentence of the prayer has been prayed innumerable times

by a countless number of faithful Christians over the centuries.

Blessed art thou among women
and blessed is the fruit of thy womb, Jesus.
Holy Mary, mother of God,
pray for us sinners,
now and at the hour of our death. Amen.

After praying this prayer a number of times, I woke up enough to question why I was doing this. That prayer is not one that I pray. Now I had to decide, would I continue reciting this prayer or would I stop myself from saying it?

The experience of this dream was far more vivid than the half-awake dreams I normally experience. I concluded that the Spirit of God must be at work. And if God was leading me to say this prayer,

I wanted to be obedient. Going about the tasks of getting ready for the day I continued to recite the prayer, but now that I was more fully awake I found myself stumbling through the exact wording.

Leaving for work after Morning Prayer, I ended up in a few moments of conversation with Brother Emmanuel. I told him, "It was disappointing not to see you at Christmas time."

His response surprised me. "I was really disappointed too. I was so sick." The intensity and sincerity in his voice and eyes was unexpected. Whatever he felt toward me, he was choosing not to be led by those feelings. I was learning that being a novice means living in obedience to constraints on one's personal freedom. However, no one had explained to me, in a way I could understand, how these constraints prevented our potential relationship from developing.

My unusual waking prayer time was forgotten by the time I arrived at work, until a phone conversation with a friend that night brought it back to mind. Jessica and I had been playing phone tag for over a week; she had some exciting news to share with me, but instead she listened to me cry and attempt to talk about why I was so upset.

Unlike my evangelical friends, Jessica didn't need me to explain my experiences in a Catholic world, as she continued to process a potential call to become a cloistered Benedictine nun. I expected her to tell me I was crazy for ending up in this situation: lots of emotions for a Dominican novice. Thankfully, she was very compassionate. After listening to me, she gave me the following advice: "You need to put aside the issue that Brother Emmanuel is in a novitiate. Right now he is also just a boy who has hurt you. It is totally OK for you to let him know that you are hurt. You should seek to find a way to communicate to him what is going on for you."

In the midst of the conversation I remembered how I had begun the day praying the Hail Mary, and I asked Jessica what she thought of my experience. What I was to do was obvious to her: "Tonight as you are getting ready for bed, you need to pray the rosary. Give this situation to Mary and go to sleep." Under typical circumstances it is unlikely I would have considered such a suggestion, but given all that had occurred that day, her advice made sense. Jessica was concerned that I didn't have a rosary or know the prayers, but I assured her that I had both: one of my Divine Office books also had the rosary prayers, and I actually had two very nice olive wood rosaries that had been given as gifts to me during my travels in the Middle East. We closed our conversation in prayer, then I hung up the phone and tracked down what I needed.

Sitting there in my bed, physically and emotionally tired, I did my best to say the rosary. If someone knows what they are doing, five decades—one loop of a standard rosary—takes about fifteen minutes. It took me quite a bit longer. I tried to recite the prayers from memory, but often had to check the book. I kept losing my place with the beads, unsure if I was skipping ahead or saying extra Hail Marys. I think I probably dozed off at least once. If I was meditating on the various mysteries, I missed it completely. But I did my best with it, lifted the situation up in prayer and went to sleep.

LETTING GO OF BROTHER EMMANUEL

Early the next morning I went to church and again fumbled my way through the rosary as I waited for Morning Prayer to begin. Once at work, though I was still sad, I found myself feeling much more peaceful. Throughout the day I easily found words to express what I wanted to say to Brother Emmanuel, and I began to write them up. By the time I went to sleep that night I had written out all that was going on for me. The following morning I woke up and said the rosary for a third time before reviewing and finalizing the letter I would give to Brother Emmanuel before the novices' tour left Los Angeles.

This process was very healing. I was no longer holding a bunch of jumbled emotions inside. The next time I stopped by the Dominican church in San Francisco, I kept my mind occupied by reading Brian McLaren's *A Generous Orthodoxy* as I waited for the opportunity to talk with him. Our conversation about our relationship was brief, yet very healing. He apologized for the hurt he had caused me, for saying he would write and then not writing, for only being able to talk with me for short conversations. And I assured him that he was forgiven.

Then he clearly explained that, at this point into his novitiate, he had firmly chosen a life that would lead him to take a vow of obedience that included chastity. He would not be free to build a close relationship with me. Taking this in, I recognized that I needed to let go.

As I let go, I saw how atypical it was to interact with a Dominican novice. And more than anything else for him, I want him to have integrity in living obediently to the commitments he is led to make. Letting go of being a bit in love with him, however, didn't happen instantaneously. Living out the decision to let go involved a grieving process. Thankfully I didn't grieve alone. Friends who had kindly listened to me share the joy of relating to Fran, and my confusion about his novice journey, were also there to cry and pray with me as I let go.

Around this time I also happened to come across information on sexual misconduct of evangelical pastors. It emphasized for me that being romantically interested in someone who is not free to respond to my interest does not bring glory or pleasure to God. All too often such situations can lead to emotional or physical affairs. More than once I have seen firsthand the havoc pastors can create when they fail in the areas of sexual integrity. This leads me to pray for the grace and accountability to avoid such potential situations. Holding on to romantic feelings for Brother Emmanuel would have compromised my responsibilities as a pastor and, more significantly, my personal morals. As sad as it was to let go, I am thankful that we did not end up in a destructive situation that would have been exponentially more painful.

Since composing that letter during the novice's stay in Los Angeles, I have not made saying the rosary a regular practice in my life. But now when Catholic friends invite me to join them in saying the rosary, with the understanding I have gained of this practice being focused on Jesus, I willingly participate. I still struggle with the rosary, finding the repetitive nature of the memorized prayer a little difficult to keep straight. Even with the beads, I still easily lose track of where I am. As for what to make of some of the beliefs Catholics hold about Mary, I continue to be doubtful. Yet if Mary is as loving as Catholics fervently assert, I trust her to have sympathetic kindness for a confused evangelical. Mentioning this conclusion to a Dominican priest, he warmheartedly assured me, "She's your mother too!"

6

COMMUNITY

Living Together Constantly

*E*very visit I made to the novice group was brief. I took for granted during these visits that I'd see them all together. Only during a visit later in the year would it dawn on me that they spend *all* of their time together in the novitiate.

All five daily times of prayer.

Adoration every day.

Three meals a day.

Classes.

Recreation.

Just the same small group of men all year, with hardly anybody else ever entering their cloistered journey. When I asked about this, they told me that in moments when their novice community can feel irritatingly small, they remind themselves that in the years ahead they will be living within the much larger Dominican community.

DOMINICAN COMMUNITY

When the constant togetherness of novice life became apparent to me, I realized that the Dominican friars in my own neighborhood had been living in this highly structured community for decades. For months I had been praying with them twice every weekday, and it was startling to awaken to this insight that had been right in front of me the whole time. Unlike the novices, who are just beginning their Dominican journey, most of the friars I regularly joined for prayer had been living in the order's community longer than I have been alive. How are these communities able to live and minister together well?

Their lifestyle is hard for people outside the order to comprehend. And because of longstanding rules that restrict women from being in their homes, I have no firsthand observations of their life together at home. However, by reading foundational documents such as the order's constitution, and listening to various stories shared by friars, I have gained a sense of their life as a community.

DOMINICAN DEMOCRACY

No Dominican lives alone. This is by design. When a household of Dominicans contains at least six friars, it is then referred to as a priory. Once designated a priory, the house will be led by an elected leader, the prior, selected from the community members. The community formally commits to a structured, shared life of prayer, meals and regular meetings necessary for an orderly household. Together, a group of priories and houses in a region form a province, which is led by an elected provincial. Throughout the world there are 36 provinces, four of which are in the United States, all of which are under the jurisdiction of the Master of the Order.

Most orders in the Catholic church follow the hierarchical models of leadership found in the church's structures, meaning that once elected, an order's leaders remain in their positions indefinitely. But right from the beginning, in a dramatic departure from this structure, the Dominican order established a democratic system of rotating leadership and governing councils. Friars are usually elected to leadership positions for three-year terms, with a limit of two consecutive terms, such that everyone is under another's authority much longer than he is in a position of authority. This leadership innovation—preventing people from being tenured into positions of authority—provides a healthy safeguard from the abuse of authority. A downside, however, can be an instability of leadership and ongoing campaigning for positions.

Today the Dominicans are the longest running constitutional governing structure in history. Rather than autocratic leadership, the elected superiors in the order function more as administrators, carrying out the decisions that everyone has participated in making. With a fair amount of decision-making power held in regional and local councils, along with regular opportunities for transitions in leadership, the Dominican order has avoided the splits that have occurred in other, less democratic orders.

FORMED INTO COMMUNITY

Community is at the heart of Dominican life, and during the novice year the major task alongside gaining the rhythms of prayer is learning how to live in community. In addition to learning the work of each priory during visits to the various communities, novices become acquainted with the friars themselves. During short periods while in formation, and then once his years of training are completed, a Dominican can be assigned to any of the communities of friars in his province, or anywhere else the order needs him to serve. And Dominican friars tend to be moved rather frequently between communities over the course of their years in ministry.

By organizing themselves democratically, the order allows for a substantial amount of diversity among its members; a proverb that has been quoted to me over and over again as I have met many different Dominicans is, "If you have met one Dominican, you have met one Dominican."

A priest from another province surprised me while talking about his seminary years; a highlight for him was overseeing the community's football pool. Apparently, some men enjoy picking their favorite teams even while preparing for the priesthood. But with everyone on a limited budget, the winner didn't get money. Instead the other friars expressed care by the time and creativity they put into mocking each week's winner. The football pool did at times create tension, of course, when a winner didn't respond well to being mocked or when someone questioned the piety of watching football on Sunday afternoons. Living in such a large community, with so many different personalities, even football can become complicated. Committing to the order entails committing to the entire community of friars.

Generally, priories have the sense of being a family—though they contain only adults and only one gender. With the intensity of not only shared living space and meals, but also regular times of prayer and shared ministry work, the friars form deep bonds with one another. In some ways it's like a marriage, except that you are tied to not just one person but everyone in the order.

A DOMINICAN HOUSEHOLD

For those outside the order, a friar's commitment to his community is not always as easily understandable. Learning how to live in community means letting go of the habits involved in living independently—giving up the freedom to do what you what, when you want to it—and becoming obedient to the community's life together.

Another freedom a Dominican gives up is individual autonomy in choosing what job or task he will do. In the commitment to community, a Dominican submits himself to the needs and work of the entire community. Whenever possible, a person's skills and abilities are considered in making assignments, but the bottom line is that a friar has to do what he is assigned to do, until he is given a different assignment. Then he is obligated to fulfill the new assignment, even if he would have preferred continuing in his previous job.

In most priories a few friars take care of not only meals but home maintenance, auto care, laundry and other errands—everything involved in running a household. Every community also has a procurator appointed to mange the budget and other matters related to the finances of a community, including preparing monthly financial reports. This extensive support structure allows priests to focus on their primary calling: to preach the gospel. Freed up from having to deal with the mundane responsibilities of life, some priests have been known to forget, over time, how to cook or even go grocery shopping. The division of labor in a priory can feel like a marriage—one group taking care of the home while the other group goes out to do a particular income-producing job.

Another aspect of life in community is a shared financial simplicity. From its founding the order has sought to avoid being caught up in caring for that which is temporary at the expense of doing the things that have eternal significance. Those who enter the order give up being able to make major financial choices on their own. Dominicans trust that the order's finances are being handled responsibly and that their financial needs will be provided for. If friars receive monetary gifts, they are obligated to put the money into the community fund. As one brother in seminary shared with me, "It can be tempting to hoard financial gifts you are given, but this is overcome by learning to trust: if you really need something, your superior will make sure that you will be able to get it."

Even as each friar individually commits to poverty, there is an abundance experienced in community. Though none of the novices has an iPod, they gather together several times a day to sing and chant praises to God. Even though individually each novice receives an allowance of only $25.00 a month, used primarily for purchasing things like toothpaste, shampoo and an occasional book, they are far more financially secure than much of society. At the end of the novice year, and for the entirety of their years in seminary, the monthly allowance increases to $75.00. As I think back on my seminary years, having $75.00 left in the bank after paying my basic monthly expenses would have been a rare event.

COLLEGE CAMPUS COMMUNITY

In my years of school before college I was an energetic extrovert who loved meeting people, but I never completely overcame feeling socially awkward. I never quite connected with my peers, and close friendships were a new experience of college life. I arrived at college having led several high school clubs and thus plenty of experience planning events and organizing groups of people. Warned by other Christian students that I would not find any Christians at my college, I started making a list of everyone I met who had any kind of Christian background or expressed interest in Christianity. I was surprised to come up with a list of thirty names! With this list of people willing to be contacted about Christian events on campus, I began working with the handful of committed Christian upperclassmen to coordinate activities.

Looking at the pictures from that time, it's striking how many different skin tones there were. There was also an incredible variety of church backgrounds, and after college many went on to serve in leadership in historic mainline, independent, Pentecostal and Catholic churches.

Several mentors taught me that simply investing time in meaningful relationships is far more valuable than a flyer or a phone invitation. Being at a primarily residential college, we all lived less than a few minutes from each other by foot. Attending that school meant that one would eat, sleep, bathe, exercise, learn and party in close quarters with eight hundred other young adults seeking a college education. Ministry easily flowed out of living so closely with others. Prayer needs and opportunities to serve were often quite obvious. Finding time to toss a Frisbee or joining a group for a meal didn't require a great deal of effort. We had discussions in our classrooms, and we continued those discussions back in our rooms. Invitations to Bible studies were regularly given. Interactions with the broader campus community were nearly constant. My mentors were committed to praying together for the needs of people on campus and for each other. As I prayed with them and did ministry activity alongside them, a vibrant depth of friendship emerged that I could draw strength from and invite others into.

At the beginning of my sophomore year I was sitting alone in my dorm room the night of my birthday. I was startled by singing outside my first floor window—"Happy Birthday to you . . ." Opening the curtains I saw a group of nearly twenty people and a lit birthday cake. It was all I could do to not cry; no group had ever organized such a thoughtful surprise for me. The group singing outside my window was a wondrous testimony to the community that had been built during the previous year. However, as graduating seniors must painfully face, college communities are not permanent. Once a student has reached their academic goal, usually they leave the small cloistered community for bigger adventures out in the wider world.

COMMUNITY AFTER COLLEGE

As I was getting ready to graduate, I remembered some advice given to me by a family friend before I had even headed off to my first year in college: "College can be a great place to find a husband," Nicole told me. "Never again will you be around so many single, well-educated peers. Finding men you would be interested in dating after you leave college is much more difficult." I didn't know what to do with Nicole's advice, so these words soon receded to the back of my memory. At the end of college, remembering her words, I looked over the many relationships I had built over the previous four years. I knew it was not likely I would marry anyone I had met while in college, so I decided not to worry that I couldn't follow her advice.

What I didn't fully grasp when I first heard Nicole's warning was how unique the community experience of my college years would be. Life after college was drastically different. With hopes of eventually becoming a crosscultural missionary in Palestine, after graduation I moved home to keep my expenses at a minimum while working to pay off my college loans as quickly as possible. Finding a job was easy at the center of the Silicon Valley dotcom boom. Getting connected to Christian fellowship was pretty simple, through the various programs for adults at the evangelical megachurch I had grown up in. But I did not find community.

As the months went by, I felt fragmented. Every life activity was with a completely different group of people. Other than sleeping at home, I did not regularly interact with my busy family members. Work was generally positive, but in that setting people really didn't get to know one another easily; our shared focus was accomplishing work-related tasks. Occasionally I found myself in conversations about spiritual topics, or in a few instances, praying with a coworker. Yet I could not settle down in the business world, and with all my searching I ended up changing companies every few months.

Then almost every night of the week I was out at a church or social activity, driving all over the place. Two nights a week I was in Bible studies. On Thursday morning I was at an all-church prayer meeting. The first Wednesday of the month I participated in a neighborhood prayer meeting. Developing my interest in mission work, I joined one of my church's mission groups that met monthly, and for a semester I was in a weekly mission class. To connect with people my own age I also became involved in a young adult fellowship group, though everyone else there was already several years out of college. And, of course, I attended a Sunday morning church service every week.

During all this a peer who had recently moved to the area asked me about ways to have a more active social life. Her eyes brightened when I told her I had an event almost every night, but dimmed again as I shared the details of my schedule. "Oh, you're really religious," she said, disappointed. I bristled. *Religious* seemed such a negative word, one used for describing an obligation to holy activity. Each of these parts of my life was meeting different important needs; if they were merely obligations, I wouldn't be doing them. But the truth was I couldn't share the fullness of my current life experiences with others. I occasionally invited people from one world of events into some of the other worlds, but this was not a long-term solution for the fragmentation of my life.

I found myself taking my vacation time to visit Los Angeles, searching for what would be next. Several things drew me there. A number of my close friends from the Christian fellowship group had stayed in the Los Angeles area after college to be a part of an internship program (like a novitiate) of living and ministering in the context of urban poverty. I shared their convictions about God's heart for the poor and was attracted to the significant community life they shared. It was a challenge to not idealize their lives during my stays with these friends. In addition, there was a man in Los Angeles who caused my heart to quicken when he came to mind. Our emails and occasional visits left me very hopeful about the potential for our relationship. While in Los Angeles I also was looking at graduate school programs.

As time went by, after making several trips I saw that the internship program was not as ideal as I wanted to imagine. The program had begun only a few years earlier, and it was experiencing numerous growing pains as it hit new challenges. Most of my friends, though generally thankful for the experience, moved on to other paths. (A few friends blossomed through the internship program, going on to serve as church-planting missionaries in various urban slum communities around the world.) None of the Los Angeles communities of prayer and service among the poor that I had visited lasted for more than a few years. As for the man I was falling for, our growing relationship reached a crossroads, and we ended up not crossing over. Though it was the right decision, the hurt in my heart over this disappointment took time to heal.

After two years I had paid off my undergraduate debt, and still being rootless with neither a stable career nor a husband on the horizon, I followed the Lord's nudge to graduate school. Once again, in the temporariness of an academic setting, I became a part of a few communities. In particular I was blessed by the sense of family I experienced in a small multigenerational, multiethnic church that became my spiritual home during my years there. But as so many others do today, I continued to make major geographic moves as a single person, apart from any meaningful larger community. Sometimes I wonder if living in permanent, stable community will ever become a more viable possibility in my life.

ALL COMMUNITY IS TEMPORARY

It is likely that people will only increase their mobility, making time together with family and friends that much more poignant. For many financially secure young adults in the United States it can be easier to just live alone. Or at least make sure that at a minimum, they have their own bathroom. Yet something is lost when we have to fly on an airplane—rather than walk across the street—to enjoy a meal prepared by friends. This side of heaven, living together as humans still in the process of sanctification, community will be a struggle.

As Dominicans know, a fruitful community is a gift from God. And unlike the struggles that recent college graduates can experience seeking meaningful community, Dominicans don't have any illusions about having perfected community life. They are well acquainted with the shifting of transient communities. Instead, as seen in the correspondence between Jordon of Saxony and Diana d'Andalo, there is a longing for the perfection of heavenly community.

Jordan of Saxony, the man who succeeded Dominic as Master of the Order, shared with Diana d'Andalo, the leader of a community of Dominican nuns, a depth of love for Christ and a calling to minister in the Dominican order. Looking back at their correspondence, it's not entirely clear whether their relationship was a loving friendship or something more. Whatever the case, the warmth of their relationship made them glad for the occasions they were together. In his final, tender letter to Diana, Jordon wrote:

> What we could write to each other, beloved, is after all but little; in the depths of our hearts burns our love for each other in the Lord, and by it we speak to each other continually in acts of love that neither tongue can speak nor word convey. O Diana, miserable is this present state that we endure because we cannot love each other here without pain of heart or think of each

other without anxiety! Thou art vexed; thou dost suffer because it is not permitted to see me always, and I, I also am distressed because thy presence is so rarely granted me. Who will lead us to that "fortress-city," to that "city of the Lord of Hosts" that the "Most High Himself has founded" where we will no longer pant either for Him or for each other?

Dying in the same year, they then entered the joyful union of heaven.

NEW POSSIBILITIES

There are a number of other saintly pairs of male and female church leaders who shared a particular love for one another. Though these

stories are charming, I knew I could not emotionally move on if I imagined such a relationship with Brother Emmanuel would be possible. I hesitated as I considered returning to the conference in Colorado where I had met Fran the year before, wondering if it would be too distressing for me. The deadline for registering was approaching, so I emailed the conference organizers about how my time there last year had led to my praying regularly with Dominicans. They replied to my email saying that a Dominican from the East Coast would be leading prayer services throughout the weekend. Would I want to lead that time with him?

Several phone calls and hours of preparation later, we found ourselves in Colorado chanting Morning and Evening Prayer, he in his white habit and I in a black minister's robe. Another Dominican, Father Jonathan, decided to attend the conference at the last minute. And participating in the prayer services was a book editor intrigued by evangelical me, fearlessly collaborating with Catholics in liturgical prayer.

In the months before the conference, my job search had continued to take me down a series of dead ends. The future still felt like a thick fog. But Father Jonathan had a specific goal for this conference: to find an evangelical minister who could fill the campus ministry opening at the university in Connecticut. Guess who Father Jonathan ended up asking to apply? And then, guess what this book editor asked me to consider doing?

Excited, yet unsure, I prayerfully considered these opportunities in the following weeks as I prepared for a trip to Seattle and Portland.

7

THE COMMUNION OF SAINTS

Living in a Visual History

*E*xactly one year and one week later, on a Friday afternoon, I was back in Seattle at the Catholic Church where Fran and I had met for Mass. The next day I would attend a Catholic wedding of two friends from my college Christian fellowship group. The only chance to catch up with Brook and Susan during this trip would be sitting together at the wedding reception. Now with two young boys, their life had become far more complicated.

Though I had not come any closer in the past year to the possibilities of marriage and children in my own life, as I walked around the Dominican church in Seattle I pondered how my life had been changed for the better by continuing to cross paths with Brother Emmanuel. Instead of sitting off to the side, confused about what was going on, I now confidently joined the Evening Prayer group. It was easy to follow along with the familiar rhythms that I had learned from regularly participating with other Dominican communities.

During the mass after Evening Prayer, I sat in a side chapel by a now familiar statue of Mary, Dominic and Catherine. Walking around the church after mass it was obvious to me I had a much deeper appreciation of all that the church contained. My evangelical background had left me me oblivious to what I was seeing as Fran had expained the various parts of the church the year before. Now, after all I had learned from my year's journey, and seeing how God formed me through it, I had no regrets about entering into Brother Emmanuel's world. Journeying with him has meant being introduced to many more wonderful men and women, including faithful Dominicans who lived hundreds of years before me.

THE COMMUNION OF SAINTS

Along the side walls of the church are semicircle stained glass windows that each provide a snapshot of a prominent man or woman of the Dominican Order. These images of people who lived in a wide variety of geographic locations and historical periods are a colorful reminder of the approximately eight-hundred-year history of the order. In my year of interacting with Dominican communities, the people depicted in the church's stained glass windows have become familiar. God has used some truly exceptional people to form, renew and re-

form the church, and as their stories are remembered and continually retold, their legacy informs those planning for the future of the order. Being around Dominicans inevitably led to hearing stories of women and men that have personally and specifically inspired me. Here's a brief sampling.

Catherine of Siena (1347-1380). The most prominent woman in the order's history is unquestionably Catherine of Siena. Her writings are so highly regarded, her theological work so valuable, that she has been named a doctor of the church. A substantial part of the novices' studies in Dominican spirituality is reading her book *The Dialogue,* a lengthy series of conversations between her and the Lord.

Growing up in the crowded home of an Italian merchant, the twenty-third of twenty-five children, Catherine was an exceptionally prayerful child who regularly spent time at a nearby Dominican church. Her hopes of entering the order were endangered by her parents' pressure to be married, and she cut off her long hair in protest. When Catherine was sixteen, her parents relented and allowed her to become a Dominican Sister. For several years she lived a life of seclusion, much of the time in mystical ecstasy. In prayer she received a call to go out and lead other Dominican women in service to the poor and ill.

Catherine vigorously corresponded with numerous political and religious leaders advocating for needed reforms in the church and for peace. Her most impressive act of diplomacy was convincing Pope Gregory XI to return the papacy to Rome after sixty-eight years of residence at Avignon in southern France. Dying only a few weeks after her thirty-third birthday, Catherine lived an incredibly full life of mystical prayer, humble service, authoritative teaching and church reforming.

Bartolome de Las Casas (1484-1566). Bartolome de Las Casas was born into to a prosperous family in Spain and emigrated to the Caribbean islands at the beginning of the sixteenth century. He would choose to become a priest, refuse to become a landowner, and work as a missionary throughout Latin America. In 1522 he joined the Dominican order.

Initially Bartolome was a supporter of Spanish landowners in Latin America, but after witnessing the torture and genocide that made up the economic status quo, he became a staunch advocate for indigenous peoples. Bartolome believed Latin Americans should be evangelized rather than killed, and he warned the Spaniards that their actions would undermine Spanish rule and ultimately bring divine retribution. His views did not make him a welcome presence among local rulers. He was, however, able to influence the Spanish court to pass the *New Laws* in protection of indigenous peoples, although these laws were only spottily enforced. Bartolome retired to a monastery in Spain and continued to write historical and anthropological accounts of indigenous communities until his death at the age of ninety-two. His legacy would help bring an end to slavery and colonial oppression.

A LESS TREASURED HISTORY

As with any organization that has hundreds of years of history, parts of the Dominican story are repugnant in light of our current cultural sensibilities. Particularly unsettling is how the intellectual abilities and iterant preaching skills of Dominicans were used to suppress heretics through the Inquisition.

With a high level of training in theology, Dominicans—along with other Catholic orders—functioned as judges in Inquisition trials throughout Europe. In a time when maintaining civil political order also meant preserving religious unity, leaders of church and state would collaborate in the effort to get rid of heresy. Many people were persecuted, even condemned to death. There isn't a neat and tidy explanation for this history. However, it's not a past that Dominicans want to see reoccur.

Martin de Porres (1579-1639). Rejected by his father, a Spanish nobleman, because of the darkness of his skin, Martin de Porres was

raised in poverty by his mother, a freed slave. Martin had a tender spirit and a keen intelligence, and he ended up being mentored by a doctor who taught him about
medical care. At age eleven Martin applied and was
accepted to be a servant of a neighboring Dominican community in Lima, Peru.

Martin resisted the friars' attempts to promote
him to be a vowed Dominican brother, asking instead to do only the most menial of tasks. Yet as
news spread of miraculous healings attributed to
his skill as a surgeon and the efficacy of his prayers,
the friars removed the racial restriction that prevented him from joining and ordered him to become a friar. Martin
was tireless in his care for the poor, as seen in his establishing an or-
phanage and a children's hospital.

It is difficult to know what to make of the many reports of Martin's levitating while in prayer, appearing in other countries without
physically leaving Lima, and even immediately transporting himself
and at times others through space. Other, more recent saints are re-
ported to have experienced similar things, and I recognize that
there is much for which I have no reasonable categories to explain.
Suffice it to say, all of Martin's life was bathed in prayer, and no matter the task he undertook, he did it in union with God.

Meister Eckhart (c. 1260-1327/8). Several years prior to becoming
aware of the Dominicans, I was intrigued by quotations from Meister
Eckhart that friends had shared with me. This incredibly quotable Ger-
man friar reflected extensively on many areas of theology and philosophy, and is a historical mentor to many mystics today. Learning about
Eckhart's leadership in the Dominican order allowed me to better understand the context of his writings. However, toward the end of his

life (and still unresolved even now), the exceptional creativity of his
 brilliant scholarship was interpreted as potential
heresy. Because of the ongoing controversy, only in
recent centuries have his writings once again been
widely regarded. A central theme of Eckhart's writings is that the inward disposition of a person's heart
is of far more value than any outward penance:

> People should not worry as much about what they do but
> rather about what they are. If they and their ways are good, then
> their deeds are radiant. If you are righteous, then what you do
> will also be righteous. We should not think that holiness is
> based on what we do but rather on what we are, for it is not our
> works which sanctify us but we who sanctify our works.

Various faithful women and men have, through a rigorous ecclesial
process, been officially declared saints. Often a person receives this
designation through their direct involvement in miraculous occur-
rences after they have died. It is common for Catholics to ask for the
prayers of such saints, more formally in a type of prayer referred to
as the Litany of Saints. Employing a call-and-response format, a
prayer leader names an extensive number of saints; the congregation
responds after each name, "Pray for us." The prayer is often chanted
when included in an elaborate mass.

Whatever else may be occurring in a Litany of Saints, the naming
of many faithful women and men is a testimony of God's working in
places and peoples far beyond the brief time I am alive. In the last
hours of his life Dominic comforted his tearful companions by re-
minding them that though his body was failing: "I shall be more useful to you after my death and I shall help you then more effectively
than during my life."

SURROUNDED BY FACES

The belief that it's possible to stay connected with those who have died is common among many people groups. I don't know what to make of such beliefs. What I *do* know is that there are places where I regularly experience having large images of people looking down upon me.

At my local government job I would pass by photos of the current city council members smiling down at me on my way to my office. Generally, I would walk this hallway several times a day, imprinting in my mind the officials selected by the city's residents to make decisions on their behalf. In the council chambers, where most city meetings are held, an entire wall is filled with photographs of all the city's former mayors.

Local governments are far from unique in this practice. Whenever I would look up in the main reference room of the library at my evangelical seminary, the portraits of former professors would hover over me, high above on the walls. At the center of the main wall hangs the largest painting of them all, the charismatic man who founded the seminary accompanied by an open Bible and a radio tower—the two primary symbols of his ministry.

Watching television, flipping through magazines, driving by billboards, and surfing the internet, we are drawn by attractive art and advertising spokesmodels to stories and people that are far less redeeming than what can be found on the walls of churches. But how often do we take notice of the people and stories in church art?

An evangelical friend, Derek, recently returned from visiting Rome. "For all the critique I could have for the misuse of finances and abuses of power in the history of the Roman Catholic church, I was surprised by how much I appreciated the churches. The art is incredibly good. And many of the people who come merely to see the art will end up hearing the good news of Jesus preached through the art. People who would not otherwise be interested in learning about Jesus travel great distances to see all this art about God."

REMEMBERING THE PAST, ENVISIONING THE FUTURE

Nothing I have viewed of U.S. churches has impacted me the way friends describe Rome's churches. The primary image in the sanctuary of the church I have grown up in is a huge stained glass window of a tree with many branches of fruit. While there does not seem to be anything exceptional about this piece of art, I'm attached to the tree from years of staring at it while participating in worship services.

I have heard many sermon illustrations in that church, but one I vividly remember still today is when a pastor referred to that window. He had noticed at a Saturday evening service that it's difficult to sit in front of the pulpit when the setting sun blazes brightly through the colored glass. During these times, rather than seeing a fruitful tree in shades of green, he saw in the smaller—but now blazing—pieces of yellow, orange and red, a burning bush. A decade has passed since I heard that sermon illustration—the only time I can recall a pastor referring to any of that church's stained glass windows. But since then, when my attention wanders to the window, I reflect on how the Christian journey involves both seasons of fruitfulness and moments of encounter with the burning bush.

In the past year I have become accustomed to the profoundly richer experience one can have gathering several times a day to pray surrounded by art. It is now common for me to wonder about how we are shaped by the other settings of our lives. In particular I have become more intentional about the art in my home, especially what

I keep by my bed to reflect upon as I fall asleep and wake up. The items on those small shelves are full of meaning. At the center are images of Jesus: as a newborn baby, as an adult upon a cross, and as the resurrected ruler seeking all those who would open the door in welcome. Adjacent are Orthodox and Roman Catholic depictions of the Trinity. Surrounding this center are other objects that have comforted and challenged my spiritual journey. Given that my journey has not included formal moments of commitment since baptism, I am particularly thankful that this place in my home reminds me of spiritual truths and core commitments.

Being in the Dominican world has helped me understand that the spaces we worship in, and the stories we tell of faithful worshipers, matter a great deal. Also important is the work of tying together images and words. A story is impoverished without artistic expressions, as are artistic expressions without a story. How we understand the stories of our past shapes how we will live into the future. What is not always recognized is the impact of stories that are not told or covered over. In my own life I struggle with the temptation to simply gloss over unpleasant memories. So I have some measure of compassion for church structures that hide stories they want to pretend didn't happen.

As I began working on this book, I was wondering about the decision to move to Connecticut. I had begun making tentative plans, but nothing was final yet. At the end of the Seattle trip for my friends' wedding, I returned to the Dominican church for Morning Prayer. Remaining in silent prayer by a large stained glass window brightened by rays of sunshine, I sensed an internal confirmation that this was the best path for me to go along. Interactions with mentors and friends while in Portland would confirm this internal sense.

At the same time, I was unsure how Brother Emmanuel would react to my request for permission to write about him. A few days after the wedding in Seattle, I found out.

NOVICES IN PORTLAND

I left Seattle by express bus to spend a week helping my former housemate in the San Francisco Bay Area, Michelle, and her husband Todd renovate their new home in Portland. Every morning Michelle and I would drop Todd off at his downtown office and then drive to the nearby Dominican community to pray the Liturgy of the Hours.

 After our first time at prayer we were introduced to the pastor in the community. He had overseen the design of many of the stained glass windows in that church, which he had also done in Los Angeles at the church where I regularly prayed.

A month prior, during a visit to the Dominican church in San Francisco, Brother Emmanuel and I had figured out that my stay in Portland would overlap with their novice tour to that Dominican community. I planned to go the church's Night Prayer service on the evening that the novices were to arrive. But rush hour traffic delayed me, so I arrived just as people were departing the church. With an early draft of the manuscript in hand, I was determined to find Brother Emmanuel.

I found the church's pastor and asked him about locating Brother Emmanuel. He led me through a sanctuary door that connects to the church's offices. The novice group was standing in a circle at the other end of the reception area,

THAT DOGGY IN THE WINDOW

A surprisingly cute feature of the Dominican church windows in Portland is that every scene contains either a small Dalmatian or paw prints. One of the nicknames for Dominican friars is "Our Lord's dogs," apparently derived from a play on the similarity between Dominican and the Latin domini canis. *And given the white and black habit, a white Dalmatian with black spots is a frequent artistic choice for a Dominican dog.*

Another explanation for the dog in Dominican art comes from a story about Dominic's mother, who while giving birth to Dominic had a vision of a dog inside her, holding a burning torch in its mouth. As the dog went out into the world, the fire of the torch would set the world aflame—a foreshadowing of Dominic's itinerate preaching and the worldwide impact of the Dominican order.

Including the dog in the windows is not only endearing (if not an entertaining "Find the Puppy" game for children attending services), but symbolic of the present community seeking to live faithfully in light of the biblical stories depicted in the windows.

talking together. "Brother Emmanuel," the pastor interrupted, "you have a visitor." Everyone turned, greeted me warmly and then departed, leaving Brother Emmanuel and me to talk. Our conversation ended up lasting nearly an hour—the longest amount of time we'd spent talking since September.

Standing in the white, spacious, and very quiet church office, I didn't know we would have that much time. So I got right to my purpose in being there. Handing him a draft of the manuscript, I told him about the project. Brother Emmanuel's first response to my request was, "Of course you can write about me. All of one's life is to be a testimony to God." He then gave me the names of several Dominicans to connect with for further help on the book, looking up their contact info for me in a directory on the reception desk.

Two days later Brother Emmanuel had read through the draft. We sat on the wide steps leading up to the front of the church and he readily confirmed his support. He even gave me his copy of Simon Tugwell's *The Way of the Preacher*, telling me it is a standard text for those in the Dominican novitiate.

While on the church steps, our conversation moved out of business mode, and we continued to talk, trying to figure out what we were going to do about our relationship. Eventually we recognized that, with his entering seminary and my moving to Connecticut, we would not be crossing paths for the foreseeable future. As his novitiate came to an end, we would no longer be in contact. Soon he was called away to join the novice group for dinner. He gave me a hug and told me goodbye, and then he was gone.

I struggled to process what had just happened. The joy of being around the novices, in particular Brother Emmanuel, was not going to continue. I needed time to allow this change to sink in. Thankfully, I did not have to rush back to my friends' home. The temperature was dropping and I knew I should move on, or at least put on a sweater, but emotionally I was not quite ready to go. A kind man walking by the church stopped and asked if I was OK. I was surprised that he noticed my internally churning emotions. I wasn't able to talk yet, however. I simply needed to sit a while, so I told the man I was all right and had a car nearby. That assured him enough to move on. With the passing of minutes, I eventually stood up and left the church.

On the way back I stopped at the grocery store to pick up food for Michelle's birthday the following day. When I returned to their home and told Todd and Michelle about my evening, we spent time together in prayer. They decided then that we didn't need to wait until tomorrow's party to enjoy the ice cream.

Later that night Todd and Michelle provided the key support that enabled me to finalize my plans to be in Connecticut for the beginning of the new school year. I returned to Los Angeles, knowing that the final time I would see the novices would be six weeks later in the crowded excitement of the first profession of vows.

8

FIRST PROFESSION OF VOWS

Making Commitments

I couldn't commit. It was a wonderful group, and being with them brought me great joy. The leader was exceptional, gracious and never wavering from the task of bringing out the very best in members of the group. But I couldn't commit.

I loved watching my small, multiethnic church's hula dance team offer its beautiful quarterly presentations during Sunday worship services. I have always been drawn to all artistic expressions of the body's movement, and the hula dancing frequently brought tears to congregants' eyes. Often I pitied whoever had to follow their visual preaching with a spoken sermon.

The group practiced in the church's fellowship hall, and classes were offered at no charge to church members. But as much as I love dance, I am not naturally gifted with things like balance, rhythm and grace. Stumbling is an annoyance I live with. Understandably, I was timid about becoming a part of the class, but whenever I inquired, I was strongly encouraged to check it out. Eventually, when my seminary schedule allowed it, I began to regularly attend the Tuesday night class.

I loved the hula classes. The teacher was wonderful. Every week was a joy of learning and moving. Yet the more I continued to show up, the more it was clear I would have to make a decision. To continue studying hula would mean a commitment to the discipline of the teacher's training. Aside from the presentations at my church, the group danced at a number of venues, including a Billy Graham evangelism crusade in Los Angeles. Joining this group would involve more than just a Tuesday night a week.

Practice at home daily.

Acquire the team's dresses.

Attend additional practice sessions before major events.

All this would be more of my life than I could responsibly lay down. I knew I was not being called to this ministry. But without any formal process for either joining or leaving, I merely told some of the group members my schedule had become "too busy" for me to continue coming to class, and then I stopped going.

CHOOSING TO COMMIT

Sadly, we can't do everything we might wish to do. Yet I have no regrets about exploring the possibility of becoming a part of such a beautiful ministry. Through this journey of commitment I began to understand to a small degree what novices feel as the decision is made whether to leave, or to continue, formation with the Dominicans.

One of the wisest elements in the process of becoming a part of the Dominican order is that it *is* a process. Over a number of years, the men who remain in the journey participate in a series of memorable moments of decision where they vow to serve the body of Christ as Dominicans. Around the novitiate are two such moments—the beginning, marked by vestition, and the ending, marked by the first profession of vows. This vow is temporary (one or two years) and is renewed as needed until permanent, solemn vows are made, typically after six years of formation.

This is a mutual commitment. With the profession of solemn vows, the person will be together with the community for the rest of his life. So as the novices are formed into a Dominican way of life, and as they interact with other Dominicans, they *and* the community are trying to discern whether they are called to be together.

Each novice decides individually in the later part of the novitiate to apply to take vows. The community's commitment is affirmed through a voting process. First, the class of novices votes to validate each other's call to the order. It's likely that the novices, having spent the previous months living agreeably in each other's company, will validate their peers' sense of call. A second vote occurs among the permanently professed friars who live in the priory where the novitiate is located. Removed slightly from the intensity of the novitiate, and having a more seasoned perspective, the community is less likely to automatically vote for a novice to remain with the Dominicans.

Once the novices are approved for making their profession of vows, they continue with the prayer rhythms, ministry work and community tours. At their end of the novice year, Brother Emmanuel and his fellow novices joined the larger community of men in the province's formation process for two weeks of vacation at a Dominican retreat center in Oregon. After these weeks of rest and recreation, the novices returned to the San Francisco Bay Area and moved to the priory in Oakland, which will be their primary residence for the remainder of their years in formation. At the priory in San Francisco, a new group of men entered the weeks of postulancy, discerning if they would begin the novitiate.

In the midst of adjusting to life in a much larger priory of seminarians in Oakland, the novices returned to the church in San Francisco to attend the vestition of the new novice class. Watching vestition on Thursday night, knowing that they will profess their first vows two days later on Saturday afternoon, the novices felt a sense of accomplishment in having almost completed what these men were just entering.

FIRST PROFESSION OF VOWS

I was eager to see this group of novices complete their first year of Dominican formation by their first profession of vows. Yet on that Saturday, as I was nearing the freeway exit to get to the church in San Francisco, all traffic came to a complete halt. I tried to lower my frustration as I exited the freeway and pulled out a map. Through many stop lights on a series of surface streets I finally made it to the church, quite late.

I rushed into the sanctuary and found everyone singing. The novices were lying prostrate on the ground, their hands extended in the form of a cross. I was relieved; I hadn't missed the the rite of profession. As I was driving to the church, the friars processed in, everyone said a corporate confession and listened as several passages about God's calling were read from Scripture: 1 Samuel 3:1-10, selections from Psalm 40, 1 Corinthians 1:22-31, Matthew 16:24-27. Placed between the Scripture readings and the celebration of the Eucharist, the rite of profession had just begun.

In his final act as their novice master, the priest who had been responsible for their formation throughout the year called the novices to profession: "Will those to be professed in the Order of Preachers please come forward?" He then called each novice by name. As each novice stood, the provincial asked, "What do you seek?" The novices responded by saying, "God's mercy, and yours," and then prostrated their bodies on the ground, as each had done a year ago at the beginning of vestition.

With those final moments of preparation in prayer and submission to the Holy Spirit's leading, the novices rose at the provincial's indication and returned to their seats. Each man sat at the end of a pew at the very front, along the main aisle of the church. Family and friends sat in the pew with each novice, sharing in this momentous occasion—a convergence of the new Dominican community they have gained in the past year, and the community of people that each had left.

A priest gave a homily that wove in each of the novices' personal testimonies of how their faith journey that had led them to this moment, creating something of a pause in the mass. No two journeys were at all alike: where each had been born, when they had come alive in faith, what career path they had been on before entering, who had influenced their decision to enter the order. Yet in each story it was evident that God was at work, calling them together to this next step of commitment to the Dominicans.

The priest concluded the homily by describing the vows they were entering into: poverty, chastity and obedience. The Dominican tradition is to pronounce only a vow of obedience; all that is involved in their way of life, including chastity and poverty, is contained in this one vow. Throughout their novitiate, in addition to studying music, history and Scripture, they have focused on learning to live by these vows. The year had been a trial experience of the daily reality of these vows, and of watching seasoned friars who have lived for years in the Dominican way of life.

Once again reminded and informed by the homily, the novices were asked by the regional head of the order, the provincial, to stand and affirm their willingness to take vows.

Provincial: Beloved brothers, whom the Spirit has sanctified by the waters of baptism, do you wish to be joined more closely to Christ and the church through religious profession?

Novices: I do, with God's help and yours.

Provincial: Do you wish to enter upon the way of perfect charity, according to the form of the apostolic life set forth by Saint Dominic, following in the footsteps of your Savior, evangelical men?

Novices: I do, with God's help and yours.

Provincial: Do you wish to live the common life with one accord, following in the footsteps of our Savior: faithful in the profession of the evangelical councils, fervent in prayer, assiduous in study, constant in preaching and persevering in regular observance to the glory of God and the salvation of yourselves and others?

Novices: I do, with God's help and yours.

Provincial: May the Lord, who has begun this good work in you, bring it to perfection.

Everyone: Amen.

Following this affirmation, each novice came forward one by one to profess their vows to the provincial. Before the seated provincial the novice knelt and, holding the *Constitutions of the Order* in his hands, rested his hands in the provincial's hands. In the intensity of this moment and the intimacy of such a posture, each novice vowed:

I, Brother _____, make profession and promise obedience to God, and to Blessed Mary, and to Blessed Dominic, and to you brother _____ Provincial _____ in place of brother _____, Master of the Order of Friars Preachers, and his successors, according to the Rule of Blessed Augustine and the Constitutions of the Friars Preachers, that I will be obedient to you and your successors for (one/)two years.

The wording of this vow has remained relatively constant throughout the history of the order, and the only difference in the vow made at solemn profession is that obedience then is pledged not for one or two years but until death. The posture for taking the vow reflects the medieval practice of a knight pledging loyalty to his master; a Dominican will be available for serving wherever he is sent.

Each man was now a professed Dominican friar. The very next thing to happen was the blessing of the scapular, a sign of both their religious consecration and the maternal protection of Mary. This part of the rite was very quick and difficult to observe from where I was seated. Kneeling in the place where he had lain prostrate just a little earlier, each newly vowed brother extended his arms, holding out the front part of his scapular. Once his scapular was blessed and sprinkled with holy water by the provincial, each new brother let go of his scapular and dropped his arms, continuing to kneel until all the new brothers' scapulars were blessed.

As they rose from kneeling, all the Dominicans present—priests, brothers, sisters and laity—silently and swiftly lined up along both sides of the center aisle of the church. For several quiet minutes of almost stillness, the newly professed brothers were welcomed with an embrace of peace (hugs, handshakes, kisses) by all the other Dominicans. It's a ton of embracing to receive in such a brief time.

Once this welcome was completed and all the Dominicans were seated again, several people offered prayers of intercession. Then the mass continued with the Eucharist. Afterward there was a joyous reception, with each of the newly professed brothers surrounded by family, friends, mentors and the larger community of Dominicans.

CELEBRATING TRANSITIONS

Seeing this process was deeply moving. It had been exactly one year since I had first visited that church and met the novices. Being around Brother Emmanuel this time did not lead to the kinds of tender emotions I had when visiting a year ago. Nor was the Dominican world that he lives in now so foreign to me. A year before, I could not make sense of what I had walked into, but now this group of novices had become friends of mine. Throughout the year I enjoyed getting to know many other Dominicans as well.

One of the things I had learned during the past year is that the usual gift given at such events is a book. With the Dominican emphasis on intellectual pursuits, a book has potential long-term value. At the reception I gave a book to each new brother to congratulate him but also to express my thankfulness for what I had learned from his journey that year. I put thought into choosing each man's book and included a note that described why it was meaningful to me and how I understood it to connect with his journey.

Beyond giving this gift, I didn't have opportunity to talk with any of them at length, which was expected, since others were also waiting to congratulate them. I sought out the novice master to also thank him for the year. I told him I would miss coming to visit at prayer times, and that I would be moving to Connecticut three days later.

From vestition to first profession, the friars had completed their novice journey. Three days later they embarked on their seminary studies. And for the years ahead they will continue their formation through a combination of academic and internship training experiences. Throughout these years they will continue to gather several times a day with their community to pray the Liturgy of the Hours, receive the Eucharist, say the rosary, spend time in adoration and explore God's calling for their life.

Sitting next to me at the first profession of vows was an older woman who told me that she is so moved by the profession of vows that she tries to attend every year. I found myself smiling as she remarked on how pretty I looked and expressed hope that I would find a good husband. The man I had most recently hoped would become more a part of my life, had just made the vows that took him away from my life.

A VOWED COMMITMENT?

Sorting out how this Dominican experience connects with other areas of my spiritual journey is not easy. Making vows to a way of life, in the context of community, has no obvious parallels in my world. Earlier in the summer I had seen other friends make vows, flying often during the month of July to be at three weddings in three different cities. In June I also flew to attend two graduations of family members who had made significant sacrifices to complete graduate degrees. Though these are substantial life transitions, involving an investment in an ongoing process, the Dominican vow made to God carries a different essence.

It is even difficult to get my mind around what exactly a vow is all about. More than anything, a vow would seem to be a sign or symbol of a commitment, and the person making the vow will yearn for the grace to live the vow into reality. The efficacy of a vow is not in the day that it's made but in the days that follow, in the living out of that commitment. In the struggle to keep a vow, the support of community—witnesses to the vow and participants in our journey of faithfulness—becomes even more crucial. The Christian circles I have moved in don't feature substantial structures for shared Christian commitment. Though I treasure the memory of when I asked Jesus into my heart, how do we go beyond this, living with others as we hold Jesus in our hearts?

Thinking such thoughts leads me to wonder what it would be like to be in such a process—to enter into a way of life with a community intentionally invested in forming a shared life. Imagine what structures there could be to guide people in this formation. It would be possible to invite people to "come and see," so they also could consider entering the journey of the community.

The level of commitment expected of those involved in my college's Christian fellowship group was not as clearly articulated as a vow, and that ambiguity resulted in numerous tensions. Being a part of the group could seem to mean making it the central purpose of your life. Those who didn't do this felt judged by those who did. Those who wanted to struggled with guilt about other good desires and commitments in their lives. It was not always easy for the leaders to challenge people to experience a fullness of the Christian life through the group's ministry while also affirming when God was calling people to other priorities.

Particularly difficult for me was the decision to study away from the residential campus for my entire junior year. The reality of my being unable to participate in ministry on campus worried some friends, but there was plenty of confirmation that going away for the year was the best choice. When I returned for my senior year, I was thankful that the Christian fellowship warmly welcomed me back.

The most startling aspect of the vows made by the Dominicans is seeing them prostrate, face down on the ground. This gesture of prayerful surrender to God is unforgettable. Yet those who have made such vows often recall not the intensity of the moment but

more mundane details: the floor's chill or a disturbing smell. Vows are
not otherworldly experiences; physical realities are intertwined in the
ethereal experience. Likewise, there's an intertwining of the individual with the community, as each of us must commit individually to
be community. There is an incredible richness of being and doing that
God draws us to discover together. Finding the right path of obedience to the needs of our community and the needs of our personal
formation requires much humility and discernment. As Christ invites
each of us and all of us: "Come, follow me."

BEYOND FLIRTING

OK, I'll fess up. In this journey of falling for and letting go of Brother
Emmanuel, I've fallen deeply in love with life lived as part of an order.
And this is a love I feel led to explore further, not one I will merely
flirt with and move on. Saying goodbye to Brother Emmanuel would
not mean saying goodbye to the Dominicans.

Yet how would this actually happen? There are several obvious
reasons I can't actually become a Dominican friar. For example, I'm
female, and I'm a Presbyterian
minister.

However, in God's wondrous
ways, doors did open for me to
continue learning about the order. My work as a campus minister in Connecticut is a shared
ministry with Father Jonathan,
the Catholic priest assigned to
the campus. He is a dynamic Do-
minican priest who lives in a nearby priory. A byproduct of working
with him is gaining a more substantial understanding of the life of

someone who is permanently committed to being a Dominican. Being around Father Jonathan, rather than being merely a visitor of Dominican communities as I had been on the West Coast, has allowed me to grow in my comprehension of the ordered life. Through a variety of Father Jonathan's connections, I'm being introduced to and building wonderful friendships with many others currently in or considering entering orders. It's not entirely clear where this spiritual path is leading, but along the way my love for God—Father, Son and Holy Spirit—is becoming ever more the vibrant center of my life.

EPILOGUE

It's Not a Program

*W*ill you join me in flirting with monasticism? My hope is that this story inspires you to start. However, because I was raised in a church culture that focuses on programs, my evangelical self is struggling: I can't point you to three steps towards monastic flirting.

Not everyone will be called to join an order. However, if we are paying attention to the internal prompting of the Holy Spirit, we may find ourselves flirting with monasticism. We may find ourselves considering how we can live by rhythms of contemplation and action in community with other followers of Jesus.

Condensing my journey into a book may make it seem as though it took place fairly quickly. However, my flirtation with monasticism hasn't been a whirlwind courtship. I've most often taken small steps of commitment. My introduction to the Dominican order happened over the course of an entire year, and much of it occurred as I opened my eyes to see the Dominicans present right around me. Even then, I noticed the Dominican order only after several years of learning about various aspects of contemplative spiritual formation and occasionally visiting monasteries. And my attraction to these Christian practices is itself an outgrowth from my prior spiritual journey.

For most people an ordered life will not be a sudden decision, but rather a series of smaller opportunities that lead to other opportunities. Perhaps you find a place near your home or work where something like adoration takes place in a community. Perhaps your friends and you decide to learn about faithful women and men who lived centuries earlier. Perhaps you participate in a conference where something like the Liturgy of the Hours is prayed. Perhaps you discover that you live near an an abbey, and you schedule a visit. And as you share about this visit, perhaps a few of your friends ask to go with you for a visit and some prayer. Perhaps you even try out a prayer rope or the rosary. Perhaps, perhaps.

While most women and men in orders are kindhearted, most Catholic orders have not been influenced by the movements that have taught many churches the value of being seeker-oriented. You will be blessed if you can thankfully receive what they are able to give and be lovingly patient with all they will likely not be able to give. It is best to assume that they will not understand that you do not always understand them.

You will probably find that people in orders are not great at giving directions about how to participate in the public parts of their spiritual life (one notable exception are those connected to Contemplative Outreach, an organization that teaches the monastic practice of centering prayer). While a number of circumstances enabled my adventures to occur, it was my bold, often fearless, nature that kept me from being deterred in exploring the Dominican world. My journey has required tenacity and a refusal to be discouraged. It's not that those in orders want to hinder people from learning about them, but often they are busy, overwhelmed with responsibilities, and many of them struggle to offer understandable explanations about the various aspects of their life to those who are outside their world. Those in orders are also keenly aware that parts of the life of faith are mysterious. There cannot always be explanations, but only an invitation to enter the mystery. If you find yourself in this kind of frustrating situation, take heart: it is a normal part of such a journey.

STARTING POINTS

There are many, many books, communities, prayer gatherings and so forth that can assist you as you follow the Holy Spirit's leading to explore monastic practices and orders. Only a few such resources are mentioned in this book. Given that the internet has been a key information source for my journey, with help from others I have put together a website to provide suggestions for various starting points. I would love to hear about what you discover on your journey. Stop by the site (www.flirtingwithmonasticism.org) and share where you are finding God on your path.

As you flirt with monasticism, know that I am praying for you. Brother Emmanuel's assurance to me is also an assurance for you: "If you long for such formation, God will not fail to provide you opportunities to have that desire met."

The opportunity for such formation that presented itself to me was to learn by journeying with a group of novices. But this is not a path I would recommend. A good novitiate is a dramatic process of reforming a person's way of life. As I would figure out on this journey, a novitiate is not designed to handle disruptions by outsiders. If my experience of falling for a man while he was in a novitiate can be something others would learn from, my advice is that novices are best left undisturbed.

APPENDIX A

An Interview with Sister Antoniana of the Sisters of Life

On the eve of the Feast of the Sacred Heart of Jesus, I visited the formation house of the Sisters of Life in New York City. In the sunny retreat of their enclosed back yard, Sister Antoniana Maria of the Trinity and I had a leisurely afternoon talking about her life in an order. The Sisters of Life is a relatively new order, and as their name suggests, the order's ministries all focus around the protection and enhancement of the sacredness of human life.

Sister Antoniana and I had met earlier in the year when she made an evangelization visit to the university in Connecticut where I serve, in order to share about the ministry of the Sisters of Life. Her inviting and joyful personality was quite memorable. When I was encouraged to seek out more stories of women's experiences of being in orders for this book, she was the first Sister I thought of contacting. Once she read a draft of this book, and obtained permission from her superior to be interviewed, we made plans to spend an afternoon together. Following the interview, I was blessed to join the community for their daily period of eucharistic adoration and Evening Prayer, sharing the day's specific focus on the Sacred Heart of Jesus.

Karen: How exactly did you arrive at this place?

Sister Antoniana: Jesus made a proposal to me. Scripture talks about the bride of Christ, which is obviously the church. But as consecrated women we really, truly believe we are brides of Christ.

K: Consecrated women are signs of what will be the heavenly reality for everyone in the church?

SA: Absolutely, that's exactly it. All of us, men and women, will be espoused to the Lord in heaven. Consecrated women are already living what everyone will be living in heaven. So it's the "already/not-yet." The Dominican friars consider themselves espoused to the Lord also, but it's not as clearly seen.

K: So, how did you end up a bride of Christ?

SA: I'll tell you, coming from a city on the West Coast with bubble tea and sushi on every corner, I never would have thought, *I'll live in New York!* [laughs] Ever since I was a young kid, I've had a desire to serve and protect life. With my church and my school I would pray in front of clinics and hospitals that performed abortions. I would go to a lot of pro-life conferences. When I was a freshman in university, the Lord gave me a mission to spend the rest of my life protecting human life and spreading the message of the dignity of every person.

My major at university was Environmental Science, I loved it. All through high school I thought, "If you're for preserving the environment, then you have to be for preserving human life. And if you're for preserving human life, then you have to be for preserving the environment." Being an environmentalist is very natural for me, it is about preserving what God has created.

When I was nineteen, the summer before my junior year at my university, I went to the World Youth Day in Rome. When I arrived in Italy I had this sense that the Lord had called me there. And I prayed, *Lord I don't want this to just be a vacation to Italy; I want this to be a pilgrimage. Make this trip what you want it to be. I want to be open to what you are doing.*

In one of the convents we were staying in, I was praying alone late at night in the chapel, adoring and praising our Lord in the Eucharist. I had this real sense that He was calling me to love Him with an undivided heart. That He was saying, "I want you to love me totally." At the time, I was in a very serious relationship. We were planning on getting married. So I wondered, *What does this word from the Lord mean? Does it mean that I have to end this relationship?* Well, the Lord worked very gently with me.

K: How did you come into contact with the Sisters of Life?

SA: At least where I'm from there's not a lot of women's communities that are growing, and not a lot that still wear the holy habit or live in community. I felt that if the Lord was calling me to give my whole self to Him, I wasn't just going to go half way. Why give up family and marriage, and all that, if I wasn't going to live an authentic life in an order? Marriage and family is such a wonderful gift from God, so if I was going to offer that as a sacrifice to the Lord, then I wanted to give it all. You know? Live radically! There is a beautiful quote from Pope John Paul II: "A young heart can understand the reckless love that is needed for total self-giving." And I remember being young and being in love with the Lord, and saying, *Yes Lord, I want to follow you wherever.*

When I got back from Rome I emailed the vocations director of my archdiocese—they're the ones who handle the initial process of people interested in becoming a priest or Sister. He invited me to come visit him. I told him, "I think I'm called to be a Sister, is there a book where I can read about all the different orders?" He really had no idea what direction to point me in, so he gave me this whole stack of brochures. There are hundreds of orders, and each community is distinct and beautiful in its own way—each an expression of God's Spirit. I was a bit overwhelmed. I read the brochures and got nothing. No attraction whatsoever.

The second time I visited him at the archdiocese office, however, I bumped into my friend, the director of the Family Life office. He had stacks of information about the Sisters of Life because he was inviting the superior general, Mother Agnes, to come and speak. It was her first visit to the area.

K: So you just happened to run into your friend, and he just happened to have all this material, and it just happened that the superior general was coming to the area?

SA: Isn't that wild? The way the Holy Spirit works! My friend arranged for me to have tea with Mother Agnes. As soon as I met Mother, there was a presence that I felt: *This is a woman of God. This woman is living her life authentically in the Lord.*

At the end of May I was able to go a New Jersey symposium for leaders who were very serious about being pro-life missionaries. And I thought, *While I'm in the area, why don't I go visit the Sisters?* The first convent I visited was in Manhattan. Before ringing the doorbell, I had all this anxiety and fear. I was like, *Do I have to pretend that I'm someone other than I am? Do I have to pretend that I'm holier than I am? Do I have to not be able to laugh?* But the moment I walked in, I felt a weight taken off. The Sisters are so real, so human, really down to earth. And they can really pray.

Visiting the Sisters of Life was like, *This is it.* I remember praying my first holy hour with the Sisters; I couldn't finish the rosary. I was filled with tears, tears of joy and a real sense that for all eternity, God has called me here. I was only twenty years old, and God gave me this great gift to see where he has called me.

K: Hmm. "I'm called here for eternity; I'm twenty." Certainly there must have been a few bumps in the road?

SA: [laughs] Oh, yes. Major bumps. Huge bumps. I left the Sisters of Life floating on cloud nine, and then went to work in Toronto for the Holy Father's World Youth Day. Getting back into the world, well, you know, there are holy men out there. [laughs] So, I'm like, well, okay, I'm not in vowed life yet, so it's OK to date. I got really confused: *What does God really want? Does God want me to be His espoused in an order, or does He want me to be a mother and wife?*

Thanks be to God, my spiritual director helped guide me and showed me objectively how to consider this situation. The Lord helped me to see that the dating relationship wasn't what the Lord was calling me to because this relationship wasn't drawing me to Jesus. I think it was the evil one trying to test me, to purify my vocation. I thank God for that whole experience, because entering an order is done in freedom.

K: Women in the process of entering an order have freedom about coming and going?

SA: Exactly. No one ties your hands or locks the doors behind you, preventing you from leaving the convent. Especially for the years of formation. It takes eight years before we profess final vows. And the three years of formation before professing first vows are ones of intense discernment with the help of your spiritual directors and superiors. It's mutual discernment, of the individual woman and of the community. Is this person growing? Is she flourishing? Is she living life fully alive? And if she's not, then maybe God's not calling her here. This isn't a failure, it's actually a success. She came and discerned it's not for her. And she leaves better, much better.

K: It sounds like you went through a reverse discernment process during the dating relationship.

SA: Exactly. After my first visit, I returned for a formal discernment retreat, and then later for a third visit, to spend time praying with them just before entering my senior year of university. During my senior year I went back and forth in my mind. At times it was clear, *I really love this community, I really think God is calling me here.* At other times I would think, *Maybe I'll just wait a year. Or two. Maybe I'll go travel the world. Live life. Go get a job.* You know, normal things. I remember in February, the beginning of the last semester, everyone was asking the dreaded question, "So what are you going to do after you graduate?"

K: And you had this really weird answer?

SA: Yes. [laughs] At that time I wasn't settled on entering the Sisters. So I'd say, "Well, I think I'm called to an order, but I don't know yet." I was still on the fence, but my spiritual director sealed the deal for me. He pointed out that if you look at the Gospels, all the people who said they had to do something else first when Jesus called them to follow Him, never ended up following Him. Those who did follow, dropped everything and followed immediately. I realized I couldn't wait. If God is calling me now, I have to respond now. And thanks be to God, I did. So after that meeting I called the Sisters of Life. And let me just tell you, the phone was so heavy. I was like, *Oh my goodness, what am I doing?* But I knew I had to do this. My decision to enter the Sisters of Life was all done in freedom, but at the same time there was this tension, this anxiety.

K: Nobody making a marriage proposal feels peaceful about it, even though they enter in freedom.

SA: [laughs] That's so true. When I called and said that I would like to apply, the Sister on the phone asked if I had been on a discernment retreat, which I had. So she got me started on the application process.

K: What's that like?

SA: The application process is actually really intense. You have to go through quite a lot of testing: medical, dental, psychological. I had never been psychologically evaluated before.

K: Well, they want to be sure that you're all there, that mentally things are as they should be.

SA: Right. And if there are issues that would prevent a person from entering the order, they can work through them before they enter. Our community, as I am sure other good, healthy and growing communities do, will help women work through all those things. We live in a fallen world, there is not one person who has not been affected by sin.

K: Describe a typical day for women in your order.

SA: We rise at 5:00 a.m., and at 5:30 a.m. we're in prayer together, first the Office of Readings and Morning Prayer. Then we have a half hour of silent prayer, typically reflecting on Scripture or just being with Jesus. Following this is Holy Mass, then breakfast. The rest of the morning is spent in studies or duties, until 12:00 p.m. when we go back to the chapel for Midday Prayer. Lunch follows, then a time for recreation, after which we again do studies or duties, until our afternoon prayer period from 4:30 to 6:00. It's an hour and a half of adoration of the Blessed Sacrament. For the first part of it we pray the rosary, in common, then we have forty-five minutes of silent mediation. We close this time with Evening Prayer and go to dinner. Later we end the day with Night Prayer. So the prayer practices you discuss in the book—Liturgy of the Hours, adoration, Holy Mass, rosary—we have all four of them too.

K: What's different for your order from the Dominican friars?

SA: One distinction is that their community is active. In the Catholic church, there are active communities and there are contemplative communities. Our community is a blend of contemplative and active. Our first mission is prayer. The active component of our ministry flows out of the contemplative. It's when we receive the Lord in prayer that we are filled with him. We can then go out and bring Jesus to others.

In addition to the three vows taken by those in Catholic orders–poverty, chastity, obedience–our order takes a fourth vow: "to protect and enhance the sacredness of human life." All of our ministry work has to do specifically with the dignity of the human person, human life and human love.

One of the things we do is welcome pregnant women to live with us. The women in our house come from all different kinds of faith backgrounds, in addition to Catholics, there are evangelicals, women with no faith, other religions. Many of these women are in their last years of college or are young professionals working downtown, and everyone around them is encouraging them to have an abortion. They have no one supporting them, so they come to us.

We have a phone ministry for women who are pregnant and in crisis; our Sisters staff the phones and will often meet with the women too. We also have a ministry of reconciliation and healing for women and men who have suffered abortion.

K: So the Sisters of Life also minister to men?

SA: Yes. In the past we have run retreats for women and men together. But it was hard, so now our retreats are primarily for women and the men's retreats are run by the Franciscan Friars of the Renewal. They are easy to spot; they have grey habits and often long beards. They really love Jesus and want to bring Jesus to the poor—that's their primary ministry—but they also help us with the women's and men's days of prayer and healing.

There are several other parts of our ministry. We have a pro-life resources library, which is a goldmine for those looking for the history of the pro-life movement and current events, from stem cell research to end of life, euthanasia—everything from the moment of conception to natural death. Also, the Sisters of Life direct the Family Life/Respect Life Office for the archdio-cese of New York.

K: Talk about the contemplative aspect of your community.

SA: We spend four and a half hours in prayer most days. One day a week, Friday, is set aside only for prayer. This whole day is lived in silence, until dinner, and from 12:00 p.m. to 6:00 p.m. is adoration of the Blessed Sacra-ment. Sisters sign up for specific hours of being in adoration during that time. Once a month we have retreat Sundays, where we have adoration the whole day. There are two kneelers up in the front of the chapel so you can go up and pray closer to Jesus. It's really such a powerful experience, a day of reflection and prayer set aside for the Lord only. Our community is very Eucharist-based.

K: What does it mean to be Eucharist-based?

SA: As Catholics, we believe our Lord is truly present—body, blood, soul, divinity—in the Eucharist. Our Lord comes down during the Holy Mass when the priest says, "This is My Body, this is My Blood," and the bread and wine no longer exist. They are taken up, and Jesus' body and blood are truly present. This is what Catholics believe and why we reserve Him in the tab-ernacle and have periods of adoration of the Blessed Sacrament.

The Founder of our order, Cardinal O'Connor, would always say that it is the Eucharist that builds community. When we as women from all over, with all these different backgrounds, come together in one house, a convent, all sorts of things can come up. It's only the Eucharist that allows our differ-ences as one Sister to another to be brought together in Christ. He is the One who brings us together. I'm not here because of any Sister. I'm not here be-cause of the habit, or because I like this way of living. It's Jesus who brings us together, and that's the only reason why we're here, for our Lord.

K: Will you tell me more about wearing a habit, the tradition and practice of the Catholic church?

SA: I knew that if I was called to be a Sister, I would be wearing visible garb so that people would know I was consecrated to Jesus. It's part of the package—this outward sign of an inward reality that we are consecrated and set aside. And what is consecration? It is to be set aside for the sacred.

As a community we wear the holy habit, first, because the church asks us to. And our constitution says that it's part of our poverty and our asceticism:

The Sisters of Life wear a habit as a recognizable witness of consecration and poverty, as a reminder of their religious consecration in this Institute, and as a form of asceticism. Sisters wear the habit in public and in the common areas of the covenant. . . . The habit includes a full-length white tunic, navy blue scapular and cape, long white veil and full rosary. At first profession each Sister receives a silver medal of the Institute's patroness, the Madonna of the Streets, and a blue band across the front of the veil. At perpetual profession she receives a simple silver ring. This ring is her sign of her permanent commitment to Christ, her one true Spouse.

K: It's interesting that you had an internal sense that was then explained in the documents.

SA: It had already been written on my heart. With explanation, the reasons were then clearer. It's actually a great freedom to have the habit, because you don't have to wake up in the morning and say, "What am I going to wear?"

K: Dominican friars go back and forth between habit and contemporary clothes. Are there ever contexts in which you're not wearing a habit?

SA: For us, no, we always wear the holy habit.

K: Even at social functions or a trip home?

SA: Yes. Wearing the habit is more of a sign for ourselves—to remind us who we are as consecrated women. We have been set aside for the Lord—and for him alone—as our Spouse. Earlier this year I was driving through a crowded section of New York City, wearing the habit as always, and I stopped at a red light. A man on the corner, a vendor, saw me and yelled, "You're too pretty to be a nun." At first I tried to just ignore him and hoped the light would change soon, but he kept on yelling "You're too pretty of be a nun" over and over. Ignoring him wasn't working, and the light wasn't changing, so I rolled down the window and asked, "Doesn't God deserve the best?" Once he heard me, he stopped yelling.

No one is forced to wear the habit. I love it. For us it's very feminine, and I think it's very beautiful. The blue is for our Blessed Mother, Mary. The long white veil is to remind us that we are brides, we wear our bridal veil every day, all day. [laughs] And it's white because we are always in formation. Other communities have white veils for novices, and then they switch to black or another solid color when they profess vows. We only receive the blue band on our white veils, because our founder really wanted us to be reminded that we are always in formation.

K: I've noticed that being a part of this order doesn't mean giving up one's femininity.

SA: It's actually been more enhanced for me, because we see ourselves as mothers to biological mothers. Cardinal O'Conner would say, "Sisters of Life are called to mother the mothers of the unborn." Our primary ministry with pregnant women is to love. And many of these women have never experienced true love, just for being who they are. So we love them, so they in turn can love their children. And what does this mean for what we actually do? We do a lot of things that mothers do, keeping the house clean, cooking meals, making things beautiful. In our charism, we show love in little ways, making things beautiful.

K: Can you define *charism*?

SA: "Charism" means a gift of the Holy Spirit. Different orders are given different gifts, "charisms." Our charism is to protect and enhance the sacredness of human life. Through our ministries and prayer we proclaim that every human life is made in the image and likeness of God. Every person is a trace of God's glory.

On our healing ministry retreats for those who have suffered abortion, we make exquisite meals for the women who attend. They come in and find a napkin ring with their name on it, and there are beautiful flower arrangements. Our recreation room has the best couches and the most beautiful curtains, with everything matching. In these little ways, we can show them their dignity, to express, "You are loved."

K: Talk about the rosary.

SA: A few weeks ago I gave a talk about standing on the front lines of the spiritual battle for life. In it I told a story of Mother Theresa of Calcutta; she was going through airport security, and a security official asked her if she had any weapons. So she pulls out her rosary and says, "This is my weapon!" [laughs]

K: I make a comment in the book about "men and their swords." But you're saying this sword is for all of us.

SA: Yes. The prayer really is powerful.

K: Tell me about Mary.

SA: The Blessed Mother Mary is truly our model and guide to Jesus. We look to her as both virgin and mother for how we Sisters, as consecrated women, are to live as both virgins and mothers. There is a fruitfulness in virginity; our living this way is not repressive of femaleness.

K: If a person is not a physical virgin, that won't hinder them from being able to enter an order, right?

SA: Right, a person's sexual history does not prohibit them from being in an order. The Lord can heal, transform and restore a person's virginity. So when a person enters an order, and then makes vows of poverty, chastity and obedience, they can be true virgins, renewed in the Lord. In fact, a number of saints were not physical virgins. Augustine lived for many years with a woman he wasn't married to and had a child with her. But, as he wrote in *Confessions,* he had a true conversion of heart, eventually becoming a priest and later a bishop. The influence of his writings then made him one of the doctors of the church.

K: Do you ever have days where you daydream, *Married life would just be nice?*

SA: Oh no. [laughs] Seeing friends and family members who are married, I know it's not easy to be married. And the grace wouldn't have been there for me. So no, I never daydream life would be easier if I were married, because I know it's not. It's hard. Saint Catherine of Siena, one of the Doctors of the Church—

K: a Dominican—

SA: She had a vision of a room with crosses. And she chose the biggest cross in the room. But the Lord said to her, "No that's reserved for families with many children." There is suffering and crosses in both ways of life. And joys in both.

K: Can you talk more about obedience?

SA: As consecrated we take the vow of obedience, and we really see it as obedience to God, through God's instruments. So, my superior at this local convent, and the mother general (the superior of the whole order), these two women have been placed in my life by the Lord to help me see the will of God in my life. This vow is active participation in God's working in my life. I'm laying down my will, really the one thing that each of us actually possesses as human beings. Everything else can be taken away from us, but the one thing we can cling to is our will. Our will is a good thing that God gave us in freedom. But when we enter the order, we willingly sacrifice this to offer great worship to the Lord. I love this quote from Jesus in the Gospel of John, "This is why the Father loves me, because I lay down my life in order to take it up again. No one takes it from me, but I lay it down on my own. I have power to lay it down, and power to take it up again." (John 10:17-18) This is obedience.

K: How does this get worked out in your own journey? You're someone with lots of leadership gifts; how did God give you the grace to live under a vow of obedience?

SA: It really comes down to a vocation to love. The Lord has given me natural gifts of leadership. And I wanted to serve him, so I kept doing, doing, doing, serving, serving, serving, giving, giving, giving. As a culture we're not used to receiving love. We feel we have to earn love, or do something to deserve love.

K: That we're supposed to be totally self-sufficient?

SA: Yes, that we have to be independent, isolated from everybody and not have to rely on anybody. It goes against the dignity of our being human. We need to understand that we are made in the image of God. And, if we're made in the image of God, who is God? God is love. God is Father, Son and

Holy Spirit, in a communion, constantly pouring out Himself into another, never being empty because the Other is always being poured into Him.

Every act of obedience has to be an act of love for Jesus, no matter how mundane or how adverse it may be to my natural instincts or my natural gifts. Obviously, if I'm asked to do something I think I cannot do, I'm obliged to dialogue about that. It's active obedience, in the sense of communicating with my superior, developing a relationship with her of understanding and allowing her to understand me. It's all in friendship, in relationships of love. I often have to renew this act of love, remembering that *I am here because of You, Lord, I am responding because of You. I'm getting up in the morning, when I don't want to, out of obedience, because I love You.*

K: Communities of Dominican men get mad at each other and then forget about it. When they spend time in community together, it's not always heartfelt emotional connections; they do football pools. How are relationships and communication different in a community of women?

SA: It is really different. Just as the friars don't stop being men–I thought the football pool story was really funny–we don't stop being women. We're more sensitive, more nurturing, thoughtful, caring. Not that men aren't these things, but the natural gifts that the Lord has given women, we have these.

K: Because you're women, is there a lot of communication?

SA: Yes, it's needed because there can be a lot of misunderstanding, or holding things in your mind. An example might be someone saying something that hurt me, but they didn't realize it hurt me. If I were male, I would probably just forget about it and move on to the next thing. But as a woman, in justice to myself and to the other person, after praying about it, I need to let her know how I was hurt by what she said. So things in the world that I would have been able to forget about or run away from, living in an order I have to communicate better. And I have to be honest, not just put on a smiling face. That's how community is built, in truth, in honesty, in love.

K: Tell me more about your name, Sister Antoniana. Why was that name chosen when you entered the novitiate?

SA: St. Anthony of Padua is one of the Doctors of the Church, known for having memorized all four Gospels and having a particular strength in preaching the Gospels. I have a love for sacred Scripture, and growing up I always heard about him. After I took his name, I found out that both my grandmothers, and my great-grandmothers on both my mother's and father's side, had a huge devotion to St. Anthony. It's almost as if he was following me around. Saints choose you, I really feel that.

Before I entered I had a great devotion to St. Anthony. He was born in Portugal in the thirteenth century around the same time as St. Francis of Assisi. St. Anthony entered the Augustinian order in Lisbon, and at this time Francis's new order sent five missionaries to Morocco. These missionaries were martyred, the first Franciscan martyrs. They were the same age as St. Anthony, and as he learned more about them, a great desire grew in his heart to become a martyr for the church as a part of spreading the faith in areas where the church was being persecuted. So he obtained permission to leave the Augustinians and entered the Franciscan order. He was content washing pots and pans in the kitchen, but then one day there was an ordination service for Dominicans and Franciscans in Italy, and no one was prepared to preach. The bishop saw St. Anthony in a corner and ordered him to preach. As he preached, it was discovered that he was an amazing preacher, because of his background in the Augustinian order and the gifts God had given him.

So they sent him all over Italy and France preaching, and many miracles happened. A well-known man in a certain town refused to believe in the true presence of Jesus in the blessed sacrament. St. Anthony asked him, "Will you believe if your donkey believes?" The man thought this was odd, but St. Anthony told him to not feed his donkey for three days and then bring him to the center of town to choose between a large pile of food and Jesus in a monstrance. The man agreed, and on the third day the donkey was so weak he could barely make it into town. The donkey looked at the food, but when St. Anthony said, "Come and worship the Lord," the donkey came and knelt before the blessed sacrament. Then the man believed.

K: Being in an order, is it tempting to be prideful? To think, *I've sacrificed so much?*

SA: Pride is the number one enemy of Christian living, particularly being in an order. God chooses the weak and makes them strong. God's the reason I'm here, the reason I'm able to live this life. That's when it all works. When I think I'm doing it—*Hooray, look at me! Look at me, I gave up everything!*—that's when pride goes before the fall. But that's not what life in an order is, it's actually, *Wow, Lord, out of all the millions of women out there, you pursued me for this way of life. What a gift. What a privilege to live in your house.*

APPENDIX B

The Rule of St. Augustine

*F*rom the earliest organization of communities and orders, rules of how they would agree to live together began to arise. Eventually, over years of refining and responding to various circumstances, these would be written down and formalized into a Rule of Life. A rule's function is to provide guidance and structure for living in accordance with Scripture. In addition to having a Rule of Life, a number of orders also develop constitutions, which are more fluid and provide further specifics on the details of how they will live.

Dominicans take their vow of obedience "according to the Rule of Blessed Augustine and the Constitutions of the Friars Preachers." Dominic selected the Rule of St. Augustine in large part because it was the shortest and most flexible rule in existence at that time. The rule is associated with a community formed by Augustine of Hippo in the fourth century that was committed to rhythms of prayer and study, and shared financial simplicity. Though the literary style of the Rule of St. Augustine is not contemporary, the wisdom it contains about how to live well in community remains profoundly instructive for our context today.

1. PURPOSE AND BASIS OF COMMON LIFE
Before all else, dear brothers, love God and then your neighbor, because

these are the chief commandments given to us.

1. The following are the precepts we order you living in the monastery to observe.

2. The main purpose for you having come together is to live harmoniously in your house, intent upon God in oneness of mind and heart.

3. Call nothing your own, but let everything be yours in common. Food and clothing shall be distributed to each of you by your superior, not equally to all, for all do not enjoy equal health, but rather according to each one's need. For so you read in the Acts of the Apostles that they had all things in common and distribution was made to each one according to each one's need (4:32, 35).

4. Those who owned something in the world should be careful in wanting to share it in common once they have entered the monastery.

5. But they who owned nothing should not look for those things in the monastery that they were unable to have in the world. Nevertheless, they are to be given all that their health requires even if, during their time in the world, poverty made it impossible for them to find the very necessities of life. And those should not consider themselves fortunate because they have found the kind of food and clothing which they were unable to find in the world.

6. And let them not hold their heads high, because they associate with people whom they did not dare to approach in the world, but let them rather lift up their hearts and not seek after what is vain and earthly. Otherwise, monasteries will come to serve a useful purpose for the rich and not the poor, if the rich are made humble there and the poor are puffed up with pride.

7. The rich, for their part, who seemed important in the world, must not look down upon their brothers who have come into this holy brotherhood from a condition of poverty. They should seek to glory in the fellowship of poor brothers rather than in the reputation of rich relatives. They should neither be elated if they have contributed a part of their wealth to the common life, nor take more pride in sharing their riches with the monastery

than if they were to enjoy them in the world. Indeed, every other kind of sin has to do with the commission of evil deeds, whereas pride lurks even in good works in order to destroy them. And what good is it to scatter one's wealth abroad by giving to the poor, even to become poor oneself, when the unhappy soul is thereby more given to pride in despising riches than it had been in possessing them?

8. Let all of you then live together in oneness of mind and heart, mutually honoring God in yourselves, whose temples you have become.

2. PRAYER

1. Be assiduous in prayer (Col 4:2), at the hours and times appointed.

2. In the Oratory no one should do anything other than that for which was intended and from which it also takes its name. Consequently, if there are some who might wish to pray there during their free time, even outside the hours appointed, they should not be hindered by those who think something else must be done there.

3. When you pray to God in Psalms and hymns, think over in your hearts the words that come from your lips.

4. Chant only what is prescribed for chant; moreover, let nothing be chanted unless it is so prescribed.

3. MODERATION AND SELF-DENIAL

1. Subdue the flesh, so far as your health permits, by fasting and abstinence from food and drink. However, when someone is unable to fast, he should still take no food outside mealtimes unless he is ill.

2. When you come to table, listen until you leave to what is the custom to read, without disturbance or strife. Let not your mouths alone take nourishment but let your hearts too hunger for the words of God.

3. If those in more delicate health from their former way of life are treated differently in the matter of food, this should not be a source of annoyance to the others or appear unjust in the eyes of those who owe their stronger health to different habits of life. Nor should the healthier brothers deem them more fortunate for having food which they do not have, but rather

consider themselves fortunate for having the good health which the others do not enjoy.

4. And if something in the way of food, clothing, and bedding is given to those coming to the monastery from a more genteel way of life, which is not given to those who are stronger, and therefore happier, then these latter ought to consider how far these others have come in passing from their life in the world down to this life of ours, though they have been unable to reach the level of frugality common to the stronger brothers. Nor should all want to receive what they see given in larger measure to the few, not as a token of honor, but as a help to support them in their weakness. This would give rise to a deplorable disorder—that in the monastery, where the rich are coming to bear as much hardship as they can, the poor are turning to a more genteel way of life.

5. And just as the sick must take less food to avoid discomfort, so too, after their illness, they are to receive the kind of treatment that will quickly restore their strength, even though they come from a life of extreme poverty. Their more recent illness has, as it were, afforded them what accrued to the rich as part of their former way of life. But when they have recovered their former strength, they should go back to their happier way of life which, because their needs are fewer, is all the more in keeping with God's servants. Once in good health, they must not become slaves to the enjoyment of food which was necessary to sustain them in their illness. For it is better to suffer a little want than to have too much.

4. SAFEGUARDING CHASTITY, AND FRATERNAL CORRECTION

1. There should be nothing about your clothing to attract attention. Besides, you should not seek to please by your apparel, but by a good life.

2. Whenever you go out, walk together, and when you reach your destination, stay together.

3. In your walk, deportment, and in all actions, let nothing occur to give offense to anyone who sees you, but only what becomes your holy state of life.

4. Although your eyes may chance to rest upon some woman or other, you must not fix your gaze upon any woman. Seeing women when you go out is not forbidden, but it is sinful to desire them or to wish them to desire you, for it is not by tough or passionate feeling alone but by one's gaze also that lustful desires mutually arise. And do not say that your hearts are pure if there is immodesty of the eye, because the unchaste eye carries the message of an impure heart. And when such hearts disclose their unchaste desires in a mutual gaze, even without saying a word, then it is that chastity suddenly goes out of their life, even though their bodies remain unsullied by unchaste acts.

5. And whoever fixes his gaze upon a woman and likes to have hers fixed upon him must not suppose that others do not see what he is doing. He is very much seen, even by those he thinks do not see him. But suppose all this escapes the notice of man—what will he do about God who sees from on high and from whom nothing is hidden? Or are we to imagine that he does not see because he sees with a patience as great as his wisdom? Let the religious man then have such fear of God that he will not want to be an occasion of sinful pleasure to a woman. Ever mindful that God sees all things, let him not desire to look at a woman lustfully. For it is on this point that fear of the Lord is recommended, where it is written: An abomination to the Lord is he who fixes his gaze (Prov 27:20).

6. So when you are together in church and anywhere else where women are present, exercise a mutual care over purity of life. Thus, by mutual vigilance over one another will God, who dwells in you, grant you his protection.

7. If you notice in someone of your brothers this wantonness of the eye, of which I am speaking, admonish him at once so that the beginning of evil will not grow more serious but will be promptly corrected.

8. But if you see him doing the same thing again on some other day, even after your admonition, then whoever had occasion to discover this must report him as he would a wounded man in need of treatment. But let the offense first be pointed out to two or three so that he can be proven guilty on the testimony of these two or three and be punished with due severity. And do not charge yourselves with ill-will when you bring this offense to light.

Indeed, yours is the greater blame if you allow your brothers to be lost through your silence when you are able to bring about their correction by your disclosure. If your brother, for example, were suffering a bodily wound that he wanted to hide for fear of undergoing treatment, would it not be cruel of you to remain silent and a mercy on your part to make this known? How much greater then is your obligation to make his condition known lest he continue to suffer a more deadly wound of the soul.

9. But if he fails to correct the fault despite this admonition, he should first be brought to the attention of the superior before the offense is made known to the others who will have to prove his guilt, in the event he denies the charge. Thus, corrected in private, his fault can perhaps be kept from the others. But should he feign ignorance, the others are to be summoned so that in the presence of all he can be proven guilty, rather than stand accused on the word of one alone. Once proven guilty, he must undergo salutary punishment according to the judgment of the superior or priest having the proper authority. If he refuses to submit to punishment, he shall be expelled from your brotherhood even if he does not withdraw of his own accord. For this too is not done out of cruelty, but from a sense of compassion so that many others may not be lost through his bad example.

10. And let everything I have said about not fixing one's gaze be also observed carefully and faithfully with regard to other offenses: to find them out, to ward them off, to make them known, to prove and punish them—all out of love for man and a hatred of sin.

11. But if anyone should go so far in wrongdoing as to receive letters in secret from any woman, or small gifts of any kind, you ought to show mercy and pray for him if he confesses this of his own accord. But if the offense is detected and he is found guilty, he must be more severely chastised according to the judgment of the priest or superior.

5. THE CARE OF COMMUNITY GOODS AND TREATMENT OF THE SICK

1. Keep your clothing in one place in charge of one or two, or of as many as are needed to care for them and to prevent damage from moths. And just as

you have your food from the one pantry, so, too, you are to receive your clothing from a single wardrobe. If possible, do not be concerned about what you are given to wear at the change of seasons, whether each of you gets back what he had put away or something different, providing no one is denied what he needs. If, however, disputes and murmuring arise on this account because someone complains that he received poorer clothing than he had before, and thinks it is beneath him to wear the kind of clothing worn by another, you may judge from this how lacking you are in that holy and inner garment of the heart when you quarrel over garments for the body. But if allowance is made for your weakness and you do receive the same clothing you had put away, you must still keep it in one place under the common charge.

2. In this way, no one shall perform any task for his own benefit but all your work shall be done for the common good, with greater zeal and more dispatch than if each one of you were to work for yourself alone. For charity, as it is written, is not self-seeking (1 Cor 13:5) meaning that it places the common good before its own, not its own before the common good. So whenever you show greater concern for the common good than for your own, you may know that you are growing in charity. Thus, let the abiding virtue of charity prevail in all things that minister to the fleeting necessities of life.

3. It follows, therefore, that if anyone brings something for their sons or other relatives living in the monastery, whether a garment or anything else they think is needed, this must not be accepted secretly as one's own but must be placed at the disposal of the superior so that, as common property, it can be given to whoever needs it. But if someone secretly keeps something given to him, he shall be judged guilty of theft.

4. Your clothing should be cleaned either by yourselves or by those who perform this service, as the superior shall determine, so that too great a desire for clean clothing may not be the source of interior stains on the soul.

5. As for bodily cleanliness too, a brother must never deny himself the use of the bath when his health requires it. But this should be done on med-

ical advice, without complaining, so that even though unwilling, he shall do what has to be done for his health when the superior orders it. However, if the brother wishes it, when it might not be good for him, you must not comply with his desire, for sometimes we think something is beneficial for the pleasure it gives, even though it may prove harmful.

6. Finally, if the cause of a brother's bodily pain is not apparent, you may take the word of God's servant when he indicates what is giving him pain. But if it remains uncertain whether the remedy he likes is good for him, a doctor should be consulted.

7. When there is need to frequent the public baths or any other place, no fewer than two or three should go together, and whoever has to go somewhere must not go with those of his own choice but with those designated by the superior.

8. The care of the sick, whether those in convalescence or others suffering from some indisposition, even though free of fever, shall be assigned to a brother who can personally obtain from the pantry whatever he sees is necessary for each one.

9. Those in charge of the pantry, or of clothing and books, should render cheerful service to their brothers.

10. Books are to be requested at a fixed hour each day, and anyone coming outside that hour is not to receive them.

11. But as for clothing and shoes, those in charge shall not delay the giving of them whenever they are required by those in need of them.

6. ASKING PARDON AND FORGIVING OFFENSES

1. You should either avoid quarrels altogether or else put an end to them as quickly as possible; otherwise, anger may grow into hatred, making a plank out of a splinter, and turn the soul into a murderer. For so you read: Everyone who hates his brother is a murderer (1 Jn 3:15).

2. Whoever has injured another by open insult, or by abusive or even incriminating language, must remember to repair the injury as quickly as possible by an apology, and he who suffered the injury must also forgive, with-

out further wrangling. But if they have offended one another, they must forgive one another's trespasses for the sake of your prayers which should be recited with greater sincerity each time you repeat them. Although a brother is often tempted to anger, yet prompt to ask pardon from one he admits to having offended, such a one is better than another who, though less given to anger, finds it too hard to ask forgiveness. But a brother who is never willing to ask pardon, or does not do so from his heart, has no reason to be in the monastery, even if he is not expelled. You must then avoid being too harsh in your words, and should they escape your lips, let those same lips not be ashamed to heal the wounds they have caused.

3. But whenever the good of discipline requires you to speak harshly in correcting your subjects, then, even if you think you have been unduly harsh in your language, you are not required to ask forgiveness lest, by practicing too great humility toward those who should be your subjects, the authority to rule is undermined. But you should still ask forgiveness from the Lord of all who knows with what deep affection you love even those whom you might happen to correct with undue severity. Besides, you are to love another with a spiritual rather than an earthly love.

7. GOVERNANCE AND OBEDIENCE

1. The superior should be obeyed as a father with the respect due him so as not to offend God in his person, and, even more so, the priest who bears responsibility for you all.

2. But it shall pertain chiefly to the superior to see that these precepts are all observed and, if any point has been neglected, to take care that the transgression is not carelessly overlooked but is punished and corrected. In doing so, he must refer whatever exceeds the limit and power of his office, to the priest who enjoys greater authority among you.

3. The superior, for his part, must not think himself fortunate in his exercise of authority but in his role as one serving you in love. In your eyes he shall hold the first place among you by the dignity of his office, but in fear before God he shall be as the least among you. He must show himself as an

example of good works toward all. Let him admonish the unruly, cheer the fainthearted, support the weak, and be patient toward all (1 Thess 5:14). Let him uphold discipline while instilling fear. And though both are necessary, he should strive to be loved by you rather than feared, ever mindful that he must give an account of you to God.

4. It is by being more obedient, therefore, that you show mercy not only toward yourselves but also toward the superior whose higher rank among you exposes him all the more to greater peril.

8. OBSERVANCE OF THE RULE

1. The Lord grant that you may observe all these precepts in a spirit of charity as lovers of spiritual beauty, giving forth the good odor of Christ in the holiness of your lives: not as slaves living under the law but as men living in freedom under grace.

2. And that you may see yourselves in this little book, as in a mirror, have it read to you once a week so as to neglect no point through forgetfulness. When you find that you are doing all that has been written, give thanks to the Lord, the Giver of every good. But when one of you finds that he has failed on any point, let him be sorry for the past, be on his guard for the future, praying that he will be forgiven his fault and not be led into temptation.

ACKNOWLEDGMENTS

Thankfulness is a state of awe abounding from the generous giving of others. In the journey of this book, many people, through their insights, skills and materials, took the work I did and made something wonderful.

Without InterVarsity Press, I couldn't imagine authoring a book. Dave Zimmerman wanted to edit it before he asked me for a proposal. Dave, your confidence was essential for me to believe in this book. Thanks for being a hero.

The drawings in the chapters of this book were done by a dear college friend, Lila Jihanian. It is a joy to journey with you, Lila, from chatting while you passed out toilet paper at dorm service desks to driving around late at night for your senior art show and then, years later, working together on alumni projects. Thank you for using your summer break to illuminate the pages of this manuscript, and thanks to your husband for his willingness to critique and help scan the drawings once you finished them. Lila and Levon, your artistic skills amaze me.

Andy Crouch's willingness to join in praying the Liturgy of the Hours at a conference and then to provide guidance and encouragement as I negotiated with the publisher was key for my getting started on this project.

A family in Connecticut took me in as I wrote, kept me warm and well fed, even when I didn't have funds to pay rent on the first of the month. It was a joy to have your gentle cat, Jackson, always nearby to socialize whenever I needed a break from writing. Judy, Michael, Amy, Mollie, Haley and Michael, thank you very much.

Fr. Jonathan Kalisch, O.P., a ministry colleague and Dominican friend, provided essential feedback on how to develop an early draft of the book (particularly the suggestion to include more stories about Dominic), and patiently discussed various aspects of Dominican life as I continued to write. Your input made this a far better book. Thank you for the adventures you have invited me into, and for challenging me to become a better pastor.

The Boston College InterVarsity Christian Fellowship multiethnic chapter invited me to lead their fall retreat with material I was creating for this book, which further refined my writing. Your willingness to learn the Liturgy of the Hours as a community, and other ways of "flirting with monasticism," was a joy. Special thanks to the chapter's staff worker, Eddie Simmons, who explained football pools to me.

Responding to God's nudge, the Luo and Kao families provided a financial gift that enabled me to focus on finishing the manuscript. For this and all your prayers, I am deeply grateful. Esther, may God's grace continue to draw us to pray together weekly.

Everyone who permitted me to include quotes or stories from your life, thank you. Far more than the snippets in this book, the years of friendship we have shared are great treasures. I am particularly thankful to Brook Selby, who carefully read an entire draft, improving it at various points and helping broaden the discussion of who would value this book.

Numerous men and women in orders shared with me about their lives and life in an order. Fr. Michael Sweeney, O.P., president of the Dominican School of Philosophy and Theology in Berkeley, California, gave several hours to discussing this project. The Sisters of Life in New York were exceptionally kind in inviting me to spend time inside their cloister. Sister Antoniana, thank you for your prayers and excitement for this book, and many thank yous to your superiors, particularly Mother Agnes, for agreeing to an interview.

On an overcast Friday during Lent, Kim Aiksnoras shot numerous photographs for my author picture. Ericka Fryburg assisted with location scouting and helped everyone keep smiling. Jessica Myles did my hair and make-up, and her husband, Todd, endured our girly-ness.

When tracking down a copy of *Strictly Ballroom* seemed overwhelming, John Michael and Liz Muller made it easy. Bronwen Catherine McShea, an engaging Catholic/evangelical conversation leader, refined my synopsis of Catherine of Siena. Seth Murray's tutorial on the Liturgy of the Hours was quite helpful, and it was delightful to visit the Murray family's business in Oregon. Br. James Brent, O.P., kindly took time while in Connecticut for a couple of months to speak with a variety of evangelical groups about Dominican life.

As I've wrapped up work on this book, I've begun seeking to continue conversations that started because of the book. Brian McLaren and other Emergent friends have been a wonderful encouragement in this process. Todd Johnson and Aquinas Woodworth each provided valuable advice on the practical aspects of forming an organization. A big thank you to the Youth Specialties director of spiritual formation, Beth Slevcove, for opportunities to design prayer services for the National Youth Workers Convention.

Mom, Randy, Laura and Emily were an essential support throughout the writing journey and many prior years of family life. I love you all very much; thank you for all the ways you care for me (and for not being upset that I neglected to mention just exactly how I felt about Br. Emmanuel). Laura, thank you for your feedback on the cover design and for creating the Linnea flower for Mom on the dedication page. Emily, thank you for your wise and challenging feedback. I am grateful for how you support me in communicating well. You are a talented writer; I am eager to read the books you will write.

Br. Emmanuel, thank you for allowing me to write about our interactions. Though our story did not turn out the way my heart had hoped, I am amazed by how this small story can now be a blessing to others. May you receive all you need for your days ahead. Thank you for introducing me to the Dominican world, your fellow novices and your novice master. Learning about your novitiate is something I will always be grateful for.

I am thankful for the Dominican priest who made sure I knew two things: (1) Dominicans are not monks but a mendicant order of friars; (2) it would be a mistake to put life on hold for a man making first vows to the order. I am also thankful for the Dominican priest who, though mystified when I asked if there was a Liturgy of the Hours 101 class I could take, gave me one of his own prayer books. Thank you to all those I was able to pray and talk with during my year at the Dominican church in Los Angeles.

Had it not been for the vision of Jennifer Jukanovich and those involved in the Vine, I'm not sure I would have ever met any Dominicans, or that this book would have come about. The dream of the Vine remains essential: a generation of believers building relationships across deep differences to transform church and culture. I would not have found out about the Vine had I not been seeking more information about Ira Glass's radio program *This American Life*. I appreciate how it develops my love for good storytelling.

My vague interest in contemplative spiritual practices became concrete through events hosted by Christian Formation and Direction Ministries. Thank you to those connected to this network, who have introduced me to many amazing saints and a wide array of ways to be with God in prayer.

My studies at Fuller Theological Seminary were guided by exceptional professors. Mel Robeck's classes are foundational to my understanding of ecumenical dialogue and the need for increased unity in the body of Christ. Mark Branson's classes, including "Spirituality and Everyday Life," turned me toward several blessings, including First Presbyterian Church, Altadena. Through Godly Play, hula lessons, Deep Well and far more, this church taught me much about faith, hope and love. Thank you to all who have been a part of that community.

Throughout graduate school I lived in an apartment connected to the home of Peter Antheil, son of composer George Antheil. As your health declines, Peter, know that I miss you and the dear community of people in your life, which resulted in delightful late-night visits upstairs. Thank you also to Suzanne Somers, whose writings on healthy eating taught me a great deal about caring for my body.

Michelle Mortia Cho, a friend from graduate school and weekly lunch companion when she worked down the street from me (taco Tuesday or boba and dumplings?), witnessed my radiant smiles and confused tears as I journeyed with the Dominican novices. Thank you for you prayers, for being with me throughout the year in this book, and for being the first person to read the beginnings of writing it. Without you and your husband Danny, I don't know how I would have gotten everything packed to leave Los Angeles.

Dearest Olson family, I am deeply thankful for sharing so much of our days over the past decade. It is a privilege to go through the highs, lows and averages together. I look forward to many more years of shared lives. Welcome, Timothy!

Menlo Park Presbyterian Church's members, friends and many pastors (particularly Jane, Frank, Charley, Libby, Rick, Christy, Ben, Zondra, Ellen and Walt) have invested tremendously in me, profoundly forming who I am today. Thank you for all that I participated in as a child, youth and young adult. Thank you for the opportunity to serve with the Africa/Middle East GO Team and as a deacon with Betty Mitchell. Your support during my years in seminary and the ordination process was considerable. To everyone in Thursday Morning Prayer, your ongoing prayers and friendship are a treasure.

For all who were part of the Christian Fellowship at Pitzer College, thank you for the abundance of Christian community, which, though temporary, was a great gift. As my journey continues, that time inspires me to seek a deeper life of contemplation and action lived in community.

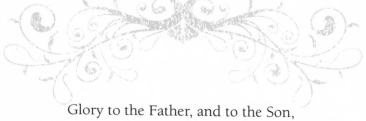

Glory to the Father, and to the Son,
and to the Holy Spirit:
as it was in the beginning,
is now, and will be forever. Amen.